THE GREAT DEFICIT SCARES

THE
GREAT
DEFICIT
SCARES

The Federal Budget, Trade, and Social Security

ROBERT EISNER

A TWENTIETH CENTURY FUND REPORT

THE CENTURY FOUNDATION

1997 • The Century Foundation Press • New York

FOREWORD

The word *deficit* appears over and over again in news reports, usually as part of solemn warnings or on lists of issues of great and immediate concern. The federal budget deficit has preoccupied the administration and Congress for the past five years, culminating in this year's balanced budget agreement. The seemingly endemic U.S. trade deficit continues to arouse great consternation in the business press. And the prospect of Social Security deficits in the next century has spurred debate about the need for drastic measures to resolve what's perceived to be an imminent crisis.

But all three of these dreaded deficits—budget, trade, and Social Security—are less ominous than politicians and the mainstream media have led us to believe. The confusion has become so pervasive that Americans should be forgiven for thinking that somehow balancing the federal budget follows logically from cutting taxes; or that the continuing enormity of the U.S. trade deficit demonstrates that overseas competitors are outfoxing domestic producers; or that Social Security will collapse or go out of business in thirty years if we don't act now.

In each of these cases, there are real underlying economic issues that affect, and must be addressed by, public policies. But our understanding of those issues and the process of achieving consensus on policy is, to some extent, frustrated by the misunderstanding of the statistics available to us and their significance. Myths and realities about the three deficits intermingle, providing almost a folklore of public conversation that only distantly relates to what's known to be true. Clarity of vision in these matters is at a premium.

In search of such insight, the Twentieth Century Fund/Century Foundation decided to commission Robert Eisner, a distinguished economist, to look at the arguments about the three deficits and help bring them into perspective for thoughtful readers. Eisner, professor emeritus at Northwestern University and former president of the American Economic Association, has a long history of cutting to the heart of complicated economic matters. His combination of intellect and the ability to write about these issues accessibly makes him unusual not just among economists but among all those who speak out on these important subjects. This volume is no exception to his past record of providing thoughtful, clear, and concise analysis of the nation's economic circumstances.

Eisner takes each of the "deficits" in turn, describes how they have come to be (or might be, in the case of Social Security), what their magnitude really means, and what long-term impact they would have under various conditions. In effect, this work should reduce alarm, not because some of the problems are illusory but because all of them tend to be exaggerated by those with an ax to grind. The oversimplified language of our political discourse only compounds the confusion. Moreover, Eisner indicates just how easy it would be, in some cases, to essentially neutralize the effect of these problems for an indefinite period. This is important news—important especially because policy decisions on so many issues are being driven by the argument that an emergency exists: a budget emergency, a trade emergency, a Social Security emergency.

Perhaps the most important point in the pages that follow is that there is no emergency. We have, if nothing else, time to fashion appropriate policies, to learn exactly what it is we are trying to correct before we charge off to change our world in important ways.

Of course, Congress has already acted to reduce the federal budget deficit to zero by the year 2002. In its own right, the legislation demonstrates the need for clarification. For all intents and purposes, the federal budget deficit is already negligible in 1997 as compared with the nation's overall economic output—mainly because of tax increases enacted in 1993 and subsequent economic growth that exceeded expectations. The panoply of tax cuts in this year's legislation may serve a variety of purposes, but reining in the deficit isn't one of them.

In recent years, the Fund has looked at many of these issues. Our Basics series has examined the issues of reforming Social Security and

Medicare as well as balancing the budget. We have supported an overall examination of the American economy by Robert Kuttner: *Everything for Sale*; a look at the issues involved in state balanced budget requirements: *Balancing Acts* by Richard Briffault; and the problems of inequality in wealth: *Top Heavy* by Edward Wolff. Our goal in these publications is not only to clarify and educate but also to help raise questions about the conventional wisdom. Perhaps nothing is more dangerous to the process of policymaking than pretending certainty where only opinion exists.

On behalf of the trustees of the Twentieth Century Fund/Century Foundation, I thank Robert Eisner for his important contribution to the critical process of reassessing America's economic policy.

RICHARD C. LEONE, *PRESIDENT*
The Twentieth Century Fund
August 1997

CONTENTS

1

INTRODUCTION

M any people talk about deficits, usually in order to deplore them. But few can tell how they are actually measured, let alone what they mean. It is past time for an objective examination of the three presumed deficits that so frequently provoke passionate political posturing: in the federal budget, in U.S. foreign trade, and, looming ahead, in Social Security. These deficits, real or imagined, are interrelated, although not necessarily in the ways conventional wisdom envisions.

If budget deficits can change total spending, by American businesses and consumers as well as by the government, they will affect spending on foreign goods as well as on domestic goods and thus have an impact on the trade deficit. If they influence output and economic growth, they will help determine contributions to and hence the alleged future deficits in the Social Security trust funds. They will also affect the resources available to support the nonworking elderly.

If trade deficits permit more domestic consumption and investment, they also increase the wherewithal to support the elderly. If they contribute to unemployment and reduce domestic output, they will increase budget deficits.

If Social Security benefits are cut back now, thus trimming the prospective trust fund deficits, reduced spending by elderly recipients may slow the economy. That in turn would diminish any budgetary savings brought about by cutting Treasury outlays for Social Security. If a commitment were made now to make benefits less generous in the future, and if people now working took this into account—a big if— it might also reduce current spending, as those who could afford to do so would try to set aside more for their old age. If this did not slow the economy—again a big if— it might result in more aggregate saving and investment, thus contributing to future output and income in the economy as a whole.

2

THE FEDERAL BUDGET

Bill Clinton, Al Gore, and Robert Rubin all say they want to balance the budget—that is, eliminate the federal budget deficit. So do Newt Gingrich, Trent Lott, and Alan Greenspan. They have all even ostensibly agreed on a timetable. It must be done by 2002. A constitutional amendment that would enshrine this orthodoxy for the ages, though opposed by the Clinton administration, was recently supported by all fifty-five Senate Republicans and eleven of the upper house's forty-five Democrats.

This "balanced budget amendment" thus fell just one vote short of the two-thirds necessary for passage in the Senate in early March 1997—as it had in 1996. The Republican leadership promises to bring it up again and again and again, despite the opposition of a staggering number of professional economists, more than eleven hundred of whom (including eleven Nobel laureates) have condemned it as "unsound and unnecessary."

Public opinion polls seem to indicate overwhelming support for the amendment as long as its import is not spelled out. When it is suggested that passage might force increases in taxes or cuts in Social Security or other popular programs, approval quickly evaporates. So what is all the fuss about?

Budget deficits are frequently portrayed as sinful. They are viewed as a shameful deferring to the future—to our children and

3

grandchildren—of burdens that we should be shouldering ourselves. A baby born today, we are told, begins life with $20,000 of debt, the accretion of past federal deficits our profligacy has run up. This amount rises, minute by minute, in huge electronic notices near New York's Times Square and elsewhere, to show how our continuing annual deficits are adding to the mountain of cumulative federal debt.

This public irresponsibility is frequently contrasted with Americans' purported private prudence. "I balance my checkbook," it is said. "Why can't the federal government balance its books?" Indeed, we are told that most state governments have balanced-budget provisions in their constitutions, and apparently live with them, so what could be so terrible about a similar federal constraint?

Whatever the costs—or benefits—of budget deficits, these wide-ly publicized and popular concerns make no sense. First, when it comes to that debt each new baby is born with, it is, after all, not a debt of the baby to the government but a debt of the government to the baby—initially to the baby's parents and grandparents. This debt consists of savings bonds and Treasury bills, notes and bonds held by individual Americans, by their banks, insurance companies, and pension funds, and by American corporations and state and local governments. A minor fraction is held by foreigners, a matter to which the discussion shall return later.

The federal debt held by the public, foreigners included, is the accumulation of the billions of dollars of past deficits, shown in Figure 2.1. (The *relative* size of the deficits is better seen in Figure 2.2, see page 6, as percentages of GDP.) That debt by now amounts to $3.8 trillion. This figure excludes some $1.6 trillion held within the government itself, chiefly in Social Security and other trust funds, which is improperly included in calculating the $20,000 every infant alleged-ly owes. To mention the federal debt is to talk about $3.8 trillion in public assets. For every debtor there is a creditor; in this case, the government is the debtor and the public and all those babies are the current and prospective creditors. So that $20,000—or a somewhat lesser figure derived solely from the debt held by the public—is actu-ally the average nest egg accruing to each newborn!

When lecturing to business groups and students, I like to sug-gest that I might call Bob Rubin and ask the Treasury secretary to reward my listeners for their rapt attention by giving them each, say, $1 million in new Treasury bills. With an audience of one hundred, that would mean adding $100 million to the federal debt. I then ask

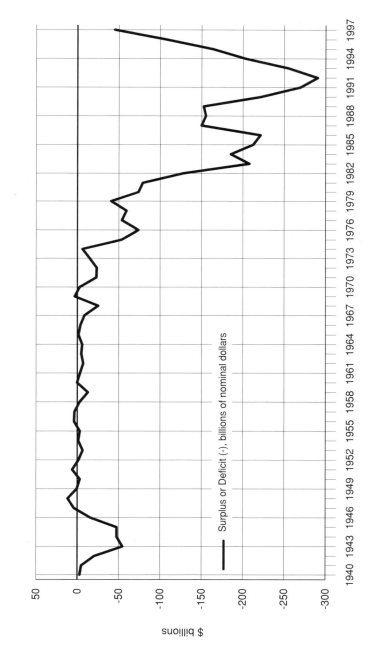

Figure 2.1. Federal Deficit or Surplus, 1940–1997 (in $ billions)

— Surplus or Deficit (-), billions of nominal dollars

Source: Historical Tables, *Budget of the United States Government, Fiscal Year 1998* (Washington, D.C.: Government Printing Office, 1997), Table 1.3. 1997 figures as forecast in August 1997.

Figure 2.2. Federal Deficit or Surplus, 1940–1997 (as percentage of GDP)

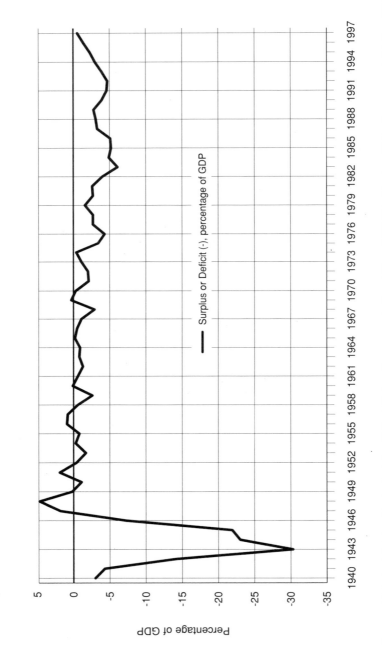

— Surplus or Deficit (-), percentage of GDP

Source: Historical Tables, Budget of the United States Government, Fiscal Year 1998 (Washington, D.C.: Government Printing Office, 1997), Table 1.3. 1997 figures as forecast in August 1997.

how many of them would feel worse off with this $1 million in Treasury bills, which they could, of course, sell at any time. No hands go up, despite the knowledge that the federal debt would be greater. How many would feel better off? Most hands go up; a few appear not to know what to feel.

Are they worried that their windfall will be offset by higher taxes to service the debt? That hardly occurs to many, and with good reason.[1] Neither they nor anyone else can anticipate when or if they will have to pay higher taxes, much less how much.

And how would your behavior be affected by this sudden wealth? Would it lead you to plead poverty, or to go out and spend more? The answer, of course, is that you would spend more. That is exactly the effect of budget deficits. By adding to the public's financial wealth, they lead people to spend more. They also encourage people to spend by increasing their disposable income over what it would be if the government financed its spending entirely by taxes instead of by borrowing, too. Whether this increased spending by the public is good or bad is something else to be examined.

As to the notion that we "balance our checkbooks," when we do, most of us do it by borrowing. We borrow to buy homes, we borrow to send our children to college, and we borrow to buy automobiles, VCRs, and all kinds of durable goods. Businesses borrow; the financial pages of the *Wall Street Journal* list hundreds of corporate bonds in the market. Without borrowing or selling equity stakes, business investment, so widely viewed as a mainspring of growth and progress, would be far less. And all those state and local governments with constitutional requirements must balance only their operating budgets. They are free to borrow vast sums to build roads, schools, and sewage treatment plants and to invest in capital projects generally.

Public opinion does not usually deem all this public and private borrowing evil. Nor do people even bestow on it the label of "deficit." But the weird nature—something that is widely ignored—of federal accounting is that such borrowing constitutes a deficit when the U.S. government does it.

Another popular complaint about the federal budget deficit is that, by adding to the national debt, it contributes to the huge interest burden of the Treasury. Again, the argument is laced with misleading figures and bad arithmetic. First, the numbers for gross interest payments are frequently invoked, ignoring the fact that the government is a substantial lender as well as borrower. Gross interest payments were anticipated to run to $366 billion[2] in fiscal 1998, as opposed to $250 billion in *net* interest payments by the Treasury. Net interest payments—the excess of interest payments over interest receipts, excluding intragovernment transfers among accounts—totaled $241 billion[3] in fiscal 1996. This amounted to just a little more than 3.2 percent of our gross domestic product (GDP). Yet "net interest" still includes payments to the Federal Reserve banks, now some 10 percent of the total, which come directly back to the Treasury.

Now, is that really a burden or something of a blessing? While some 27 percent of federal interest payments currently go to foreigners,[4] the rest form part of the income of millions of Americans: what they are receiving directly, on those saving bonds, Treasury bills, notes, and bonds that they own outright, or indirectly from their pension funds, insurance companies, and banks. Would that retiree in Miami Beach have been better off last year without $663 of interest on her savings bonds or certificates of deposit, her per capita share of U.S. interest payments to Americans in fiscal 1996?[5] Or did that year's $241 billion in net interest payments, like the $350 billion in Social Security benefits, along with other government "transfer payments," represent valuable components of people's disposable income?

It is argued, though, that these interest payments, while a small part of GDP, are a large—if declining—proportion of federal budget outlays, making up almost 16 percent of the $1,560 billion total in 1996.[6] That forces policymakers to starve other, more useful beneficiaries of government outlays: education, health, research, and infrastructure.

There may be something to this argument, but it is more a matter of foolish politics than economics. Without the above-mentioned interest receipts, the public would have still less income with which to pay taxes, and it might object all the more to outlays that seem to raise them. Ultimately, the important thing is harnessing all of the nation's productive resources and utilizing them wisely. Interest payments on the debt, unlike payments that recruit more police, hire more teachers, or build more roads, which may redirect the output of goods and services, are not a direct claim on our productive resources. If financed by taxes, interest payments are a wash: the taxes reduce disposable income by the amount that the interest payments add, and there is no net claim on the nation's resources, and no direct effect on the nation's output.

A companion argument excoriating interest payments is that if the United States continues to run budget deficits they will ultimately absorb all of our budget and a much larger proportion of our GDP than today's relatively minor 3 percent. But this is once again bad arithmetic that ignores the continued growth of both the budget and GDP. The fact is that if debt does not grow faster than the GDP, and if interest rates remain the same, the ratio of interest payments to GDP cannot rise. Similarly, if the debt does not grow faster than the budget, the ratio of interest payments to total outlays cannot rise.

This leads to the very pertinent question of what constitutes "balance" in a moving economy. A person standing in one place and not moving may be in perfect balance. Yet in reality that person is moving with the surface of the earth at a clip of perhaps 17,000 miles a day—depending on the latitude—and the earth itself is dashing around the sun at a speed of about 1.6 million miles a day, not to mention the movement of the sun within our galaxy and the movement of our galaxy itself. The point, of course, is that change, and balance, must be relative to something. The meaningful relation for deficits and debt is to income.

When an individual goes to a bank to borrow, the key question the lending officer asks is, "What is your income?" Current and prospective income must be sufficient to permit servicing the loan. Your parents may have owed $50,000 on their home mortgage, and you may owe $100,000. But if their income was $20,000 a year and your income is $50,000 a year, your debt is *relatively* less. And so it is with the federal debt.

In 1946, just after World War II, the federal debt held by the public was $242 billion, as shown in Figure 2.3 (see page 10). At the end of the 1996 fiscal year, that figure was $3,733 billion. But in 1946 that debt came to 111 percent of GDP, while in 1996 it equaled 50 percent (see Figure 2.4, page 11). Which debt was higher? Which debt was more of a burden, or blessing?

Some simple but fundamental arithmetic, widely ignored or not understood, makes clear that the country can run a substantial, permanent deficit without raising the ratio of debt to income or GDP. As a general rule, if the ratio of the deficit to GDP equals the rate of growth of GDP multiplied by the ratio of the debt to GDP, the debt-to-GDP ratio will remain constant. Even assuming, conservatively, that the GDP grows at a rate of only 5 percent (nominally, since debt

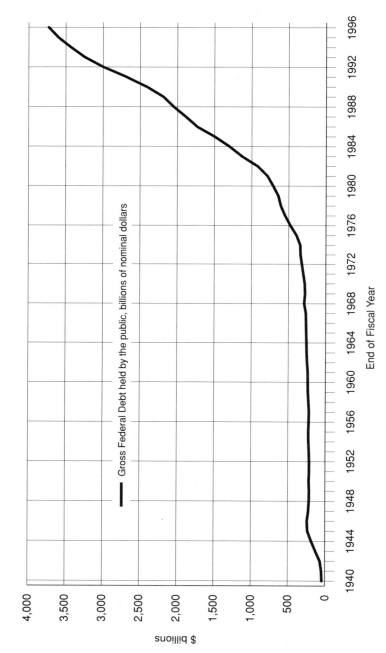

Figure 2.3. Gross Federal Debt Held by the Public, 1940–1996 (in $ billions)

Gross Federal Debt held by the public, billions of nominal dollars

$ billions

End of Fiscal Year

Source: Historical Tables, Budget of the United States Government, Fiscal Year 1998 (Washington, D.C.: Government Printing Office, 1997), Table 1.3 1997, Table 7.1.

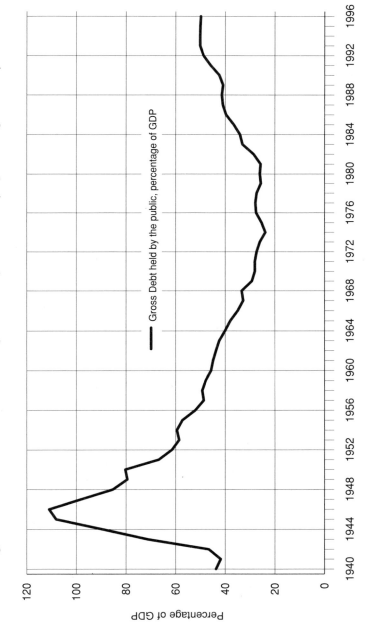

Figure 2.4. Gross Federal Debt Held by the Public, 1940–1996 (as percentage of GDP)

Gross Debt held by the public, percentage of GDP

Percentage of GDP

1940 1944 1948 1952 1956 1960 1964 1968 1972 1976 1980 1984 1988 1992 1996

Note: GDP data before 1960 are an approximation to the new benchmarks.
Source: Historical Tables, Budget of the United States Government, Fiscal Year 1998 (Washington, D.C.: Government Printing Office, 1997), Table 1.3 1997, Table 7.1.

and deficit are measured in nominal terms, that is, unadjusted for inflation)[7] and the debt-to-GDP ratio remains about one-to-two, that means Washington can sustain a permanent deficit of 2.5 percent of GDP, as shown in Table 2.1. The debt would be growing absolutely, but like the person standing in one spot on earth, it would, in an economic sense, be remaining in place. From this perspective, a "balanced" budget may appropriately be viewed as one that does not alter the debt-to-GDP ratio.

A lesser deficit-to-GDP ratio than 2.5 percent under the same assumptions would lower the debt-to-GDP ratio. As illustrated in Figure 2.5 (see page 14), again taking 5 percent per annum growth in nominal GDP, continuation of the implicit 0.89 percent ratio forecast by the Congressional Budget Office for 1997 in May (since reduced to 0.43 percent in its August forecast) would eventually cut the debt-to-GDP ratio to 17.8 percent ($0.89 \div 0.05$).[8]

There is, of course, nothing sacrosanct about the current debt-to-GDP ratio of almost exactly 50 percent. As may be noted in Figure 2.4, it has been as high as 111 percent, in 1946, and as low as 24 percent, in 1974. It might be wise, though, to observe the old adage: If it ain't broke, don't fix it. This 50 percent ratio seems to be leaving the economy with a reasonable amount of purchasing power and portfolio balance. Changing the debt-to-GDP ratio in either direction will disturb the economy.

This is not to say that the ratio should be kept constant regardless of circumstances. In the event of a recession, deficits will rise, and the debt-to-GDP ratio should be allowed—even encouraged—to rise with it. In a boom economy, the ratio may be allowed to decline. If a need for major capital investments is perceived—for infrastructure, to repair or replace crumbling school buildings, or for intangible investment in education and training and health—it may be well to increase the ratio in order to finance that investment in our future.

A deficit equal to 2.5 percent of GDP would, in fiscal 1996, have come to $187 billion. The actual deficit as conventionally measured was $107 billion. The 1996 budget thus ended in an "overbalance" of $80 billion—the amount that outlays would have had to be raised, or taxes reduced, in order to preserve the debt-to-GDP ratio. In fact, of course, there was no popular outcry in favor of steady ratios. Rather, this overbalance reduced the debt-to-GDP ratio in 1996. With the latest (August 1997) Congressional Budget Office and administration forecasts of current-year deficits of $34 billion and $37 billion,

Table 2.1. Debt and Interest Payments with Constant Deficit of 2.5 Percent of GDP and Constant 5.0 Percent Rate of Growth of GDP

| Year | Billions of Dollars | | | | As Percentage of GDP | |
	Deficit[1]	Debt[2]	Interest Payments[3]	GDP	Debt	Interest Payments
1996	107.3	3,733.0	241.1	7,466.0[4]	50.0	3.2
1997	186.6	3,919.6	253.2	7,839.3	50.0	3.2
1998	196.0	4,115.6	265.8	8,231.3	50.0	3.2
2000	216.1	4,537.5	293.1	9,075.0	50.0	3.2
2010	351.9	7,391.1	477.4	14,782.2	50.0	3.2
2030	933.6	19,610.7	1,266.6	39,221.5	50.0	3.2

[1] after 1996 = 2.5 percent of previous year's GDP

[2] after 1996 = current deficit plus debt at end of previous year

[3] 6.78154 percent of debt at end of previous year

[4] assumed value (rather than actual 7,487.4) so that debt is rounded to 50 percent of GDP rather than actual 49.9 percent

Figure 2.5. Debt If Current Ratio of Deficit to GDP Is Maintained and GDP Grows at 5 Percent Per Year, 1996–2068 (as a percentage of GDP)

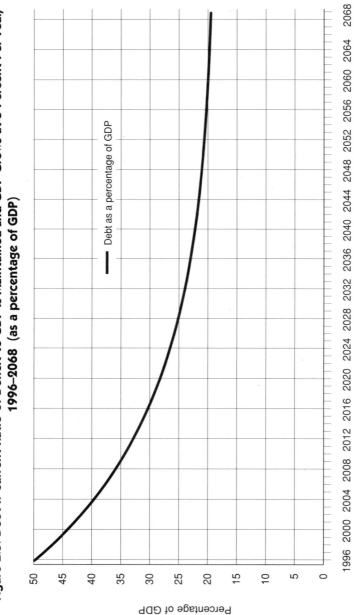

Note: Author's projections assume that the deficit maintains the Congressional Budget Office's May 1997 projected level of 0.89 percentage of GDP for 1997 and the economy grows at a nominal 5 percent per year. Growth from 1996 to 1997 (first quarter to first quarter) was in fact 6.24 percent. Over the four years from 1993 to 1997 growth in GDP averaged 5.33 percent, of which 2.9 percent was real, and 2.4 percent was inflation.

respectively, the debt-to-GDP ratio will probably fall further as another overbalance is registered.

All this should shed more light on the burden that interest payments impose on our budget. If the debt-to-GDP ratio remains constant and interest rates remain the same, interest payments will remain a constant proportion of both the debt and GDP: some 6.8 percent of the former and 3.2 percent of the latter, as noted in Table 2.1. One important way to lower these ratios would be to lower interest rates. Alan Greenspan has it in his power to bring around his colleagues on the Federal Reserve Board and its Open Market Committee and accomplish just that, as investors well understand.[9] I would warmly recommend lower rates, not in order to reduce interest costs to the Treasury, although this would be an important by-product, but to bring the economy closer to its full potential with respect to current production and investment for the future. Greenspan and his colleagues seemed, earlier this year, to be moving in the other direction.

Before the impact of budget deficits can be assessed, they must be measured in a meaningful fashion. And what is meaningful is largely determined by the effect budget deficits have on the economy. First, deficits are an alternative to financing outlays by taxes. They produce additional Treasury obligations, usually interest-bearing, although they might be non-interest-bearing currency or, what amounts to the same thing, interest-bearing securities owned by our monetary authority, the Federal Reserve. In any event, the deficits top up the debt of the federal government while adding commensurately to the financial wealth of everybody else. If deficits increase the ratio of wealth to income, they induce greater nonfederal spending relative to income.[10] One way to measure a deficit, if concerns about its effect on purchasing power or aggregate demand are paramount, is to use the yardstick just discussed. By how much does a conventionally measured deficit exceed (a *true* economic deficit) or fall short of (a true economic surplus) the amount that would keep the debt-to-GDP ratio constant?

But what about inflation? The students or businesspeople whom I rewarded earlier with $1 million in Treasury notes surely felt richer and would therefore spend more. But, altering the figures somewhat, suppose they had held $1 million in Treasury notes last year, and this year I gave them an additional $10,000. Would they then feel richer than a year ago and spend more? Not unless they were guilty of "money illusion," a real sin in economic theory and a measure of considerable ignorance in actual behavior. Assuming that there was even a very modest inflation of 2 percent over the past year, their $1,010,000 in Treasury notes would be worth some 2 percent less than the previous year's purchasing power, a decline in real value of about $10,000 (precisely, $9,804, as $1,010,000 divided by 1.02 yields $990,196).

This indicates that in order to gauge the impact of a deficit one must at least adjust it for inflation. A deficit adds to the debt; except for some other vagaries of federal accounting, the increase in the accumulated debt is exactly equal to the annual deficit. But surely, to be meaningful, the proper measure must be of the increase in the real value of the debt—that is, the debt adjusted for inflation.[11] With a debt held by the public averaging about $3,670 billion in 1996, even the modest inflation rate of 2 percent would indicate an "inflation tax" of $72 billion, suggesting a real deficit of $107 billion minus $72 billion, or a fairly trivial $35 billion, less than half of 1 percent of GDP (see Figure 2.6). Measures of inflation indeed vary. If one were to take last year's inflation, as some do, to be 3 percent, the inflation tax or loss in real value of the outstanding debt would be $107 billion, equaling the nominal deficit of $107 billion and thus indicating no real deficit at all, as shown in Table 2.2.

There is significantly more, though, to measuring the impact of the deficit on the economy. Most important is to recognize that the relationship is dynamic and two-way, and to separate out the impact of the economy on the deficit. As current debate about balancing the

Table 2.2. Nominal Deficit, Inflation, and Real Deficit, Billions of Dollars

Nominal Surplus or Deficit (-)	Gross Debt Held by Public (Average Holdings during Year)	Inflation Rate	Inflation Tax = Loss in Real Value of Debt Due to Inflation	Real Surplus or Deficit (-) (Nominal Surplus Plus Inflation Tax)
-107.3	3,670	2 %	72.0	-35.3
-107.3	3,670	3 %	106.9	-0.4

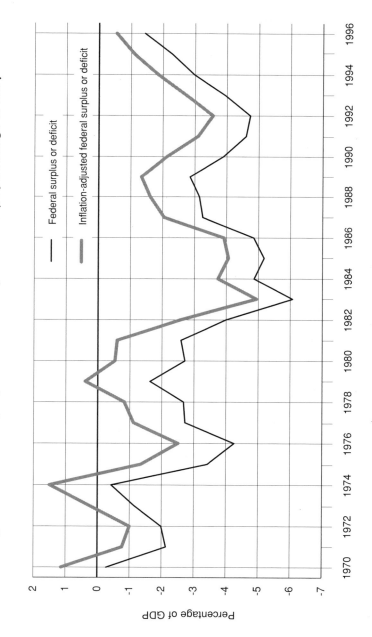

Figure 2.6. The Deficit, Adjusted for Inflation, 1970–1996 (as percentage of GDP)

Federal surplus or deficit

Inflation-adjusted federal surplus or deficit

Percentage of GDP

1970 1972 1974 1976 1978 1980 1982 1984 1986 1988 1990 1992 1994 1996

2 1 0 -1 -2 -3 -4 -5 -6 -7

Source: Economic Report of the President (Washington, D.C.: Government Printing Office, 1997), Table 1.3 1997, pp. 389–90. The deficit adjustment for inflation is based on the loss in real value of the average federal debt held by the public during the year due to inflation as measured by the GDP implicit price deflator.

conventionally measured budget makes clear, the actual deficit will depend enormously on the size and shape of the economy, which determine revenues from individual and corporate income taxes as well as some outlays, such as unemployment benefits. The huge "Reagan deficit" of $208 billion in fiscal 1983—6.1 percent of GDP—was as much or more the consequence of the 1982–83 recession, the worst since the Great Depression of the 1930s, as of legislated tax cuts and the surge in military expenditures. A recent, sharp case in point was the adjustment of forecasts by the Congressional Budget Office of the fiscal 1997 deficit from $127 billion to $75 billion and then to $34 billion as the economy turned out to be more prosperous and tax payments greater than anticipated.

Recognizing this, economists beginning with Herbert Stein, later chairman of President Nixon's Council of Economic Advisers, serving on the business-sponsored Committee on Economic Development right after World War II, have therefore constructed measures of what is variously known as a "full-employment," "standardized," "structural," "cyclically adjusted," or "high-employment" deficit. These indicate what the deficit would be at some given state of the economy—say, for example, at 6 percent unemployment. Ups and downs in this deficit are independent of the differences in unemployment payments and other benefits as well as tax revenues that the economic cycle of recession and recovery determines. If the cyclically adjusted deficit rises, the government is increasing its spending relative to taxes and increasing its borrowing more than the economic cycle can account for. Changes in this deficit are what really make an impact on the economy.

Adjusting for both inflation and other changes in the economy, one can derive an inflation-adjusted, standardized deficit, as in Figure 2.7, and examine its impact on GDP and the rate of growth, on unemployment, and on investment. I shall note the results of that shortly, but it will be useful to consider first what economic theory indicates should be expected to occur as a consequence of deficits.

In a full-employment economy where, in the short run, output cannot be increased, an increase in expenditures can only result in higher prices. Thus, a real budget deficit, to the extent that it induces more private spending as suggested above, will have as its initial effect inflation. Contrary to the conventional economic wisdom, however, more real consumer spending need not be at the expense of saving and investment for our future. Increases in consumer spending will induce business to use its share of the greater financial wealth to meet increased

Figure 2.7. The Cyclically Adjusted and Inflation-Adjusted Budget Deficits, 1970–1996 (as percentage of GDP)

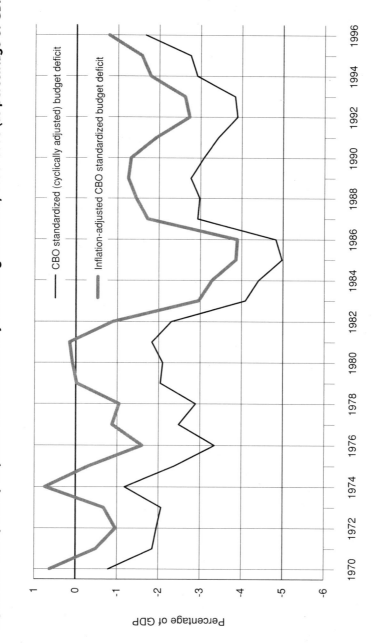

Legend:
- CBO standardized (cyclically adjusted) budget deficit
- Inflation-adjusted CBO standardized budget deficit

Source: Congressional Budget Office, *The Economic and Budget Outlook, Fiscal years 1997–2006* (Washington, D.C.: Government Printing Office, 1996), Table 1.3 1997, Table A-1, pp. 100–101, updated and adjusted by the CBO and author's calculations.

consumer demand with more investment in plant and equipment so it can produce more. When the economy is operating at full capacity, however, this will only make the inflation general, encompassing these investment goods as well as consumer goods. Consumer and investment good prices should rise alike.

If the monetary authority—our Federal Reserve—seeks to counter this inflation by tightening credit and raising interest rates, that will constrain investment, not only business and nonprofit investment in plant and equipment but household investment in housing and durable goods, and public, bond-financed capital outlays for schools and infrastructure. The problem here, though, is not the deficit itself but the monetary response to it.

If the Fed were to accommodate the deficit, however, allowing the money supply to increase sufficiently for real interest rates to remain unchanged, the scenario would be different. While the nominal deficit would continue, the higher rate of inflation would raise the inflation tax on outstanding government debt. Inflation would keep increasing, and with it the inflation tax, until the real deficit declined to zero or to the level, in a growing economy, that would keep the debt-GDP ratio constant.[12] There would be, as a first approximation, no change of any great economic magnitude. I insert "as a first approximation" because there is one factor that would suggest some increase in investment. This would stem from what is known as the Tobin-Mundell effect,[13] which indicates that rising prices should induce some move to substitute goods for wealth fixed in money terms, and hence increase the amount of capital stock.

Under conditions of less than full employment, the story is quite different. Since more people and idle resources can be put to work, more can and will be produced if there is more purchasing power and greater demand. Real deficits, adding to private financial wealth, have exactly this effect. They induce more production, very likely even at the outset, of both consumer and investment goods. If the initial stimulus is only to consumption, however, the need to expand facilities to produce more consumer goods provokes more investment as well. Of course, the increased demand and investment in particular can be choked off by tighter money and higher interest rates in the name of keeping prices in check. There is little excuse for this, however. As long as there is significant unemployment and idle resources, increases in production need not and generally do not have any substantial effect toward increasing inflation.

There is, to be sure, a widely accepted dogma of the "NAIRU," or non-accelerating-inflation rate of unemployment, which proclaims that when unemployment drops below a certain point (not necessarily one of full employment), inflation will accelerate. It will not merely move to a higher level but will keep on increasing indefinitely—2, 4, 7, 11, 20 percent and ever upward. Acceptance of this dogma has apparently led the Federal Reserve to increase interest rates a number of times when unemployment was still substantial but below or threatening to dip below this trapdoor to doomsday. The NAIRU was long believed by many of its acolytes to be 6 percent, while conservatives such as Martin Feldstein, president of the prestigious National Bureau of Economic Research and formerly chairman of the Council of Economic Advisers to President Reagan, suggested it was even higher, perhaps 6.5 to 7 percent.

My own work in recent years suggests that if there is a NAIRU, the effects of straying from it are not symmetrical.[14] That is, high unemployment does seem to reduce inflation, but low unemployment, unless it is driven to truly minuscule levels like 2 or 3 percent in the United States, does not appear to have raised inflation. Other economists have also challenged the applicability if not the very concept of the NAIRU.[15] And contemporary experience offers a striking confirmation of our criticisms. Unemployment has now been below that heretofore crucial 6 percent since September 1994, falling in May and again in July 1997 to 4.8 percent, its lowest in nearly twenty-four years, while inflation has not increased; by most measures it has apparently declined. One of the leading promoters of the NAIRU, Robert J. Gordon, who had long estimated 6 percent unemployment as the critical rate, has now come up with a "time-varying" NAIRU,[16] indicating that by the middle of 1996 this measure had fallen to perhaps as low as 5.4 percent.[17] His "TV-NAIRU" has the convenient property of continuing to drop as events demonstrate that inflation is not accelerating despite unemployment persistently below the previously estimated NAIRU; perhaps Gordon would now estimate it at the actual August unemployment rate of 4.9 percent. Alan Greenspan, happily, has expressed his own doubts about the NAIRU, and there is hope that the influence of this doctrine on U.S. policy is receding.

Deficits can be too large if they generate aggregate demand or spending in excess of what can be produced at current price levels. They then bring increased inflation, not usually the disaster it is made out to be in some quarters but hardly an outcome to be desired. What is worse, the usual attempted cure for inflation, tight money that raises interest rates, may be worse than the disease because it reduces investment.

Under the fairly general condition of an economy at less than full employment with unused capacity for additional output, however, deficits are usually more helpful. Real budget deficits, if not counterbalanced by tight monetary policy and higher interest rates, are likely to expand the economy, increase GDP and its rate of growth, boost investment as well as consumption, and reduce unemployment. I have demonstrated precisely this relationship in a series of papers and books over a number of years. Data for the U.S. economy since 1955 show a clear pattern of this stimulatory effect.[18] Larger, inflation-adjusted, high-employment deficits, illustrated in Figure 2.8, have been associated with more rapid subsequent growth of real GDP. Since more output requires more workers, as might be expected the larger budget deficits were also accompanied by reductions in unemployment. Lesser deficits or larger surpluses were thus associated with subsequent increases in unemployment as can be seen clearly with the naked eye in Figure 2.9 (see page 24).[19] They were associated not only with higher consumption but with more gross private domestic investment as well.

In one analysis[20] I found that each percentage point of this deficit was associated with an average of about three-quarters of a percentage point more in subsequent gross private domestic investment, both measured as ratios of GDP. The effect of inflation-adjusted, high-employment budget deficits on *total* gross private investment was different, however, because they were associated with less net foreign investment; one percentage point more of deficit was matched by one-quarter to four-tenths of a percentage point less of net foreign investment.

This was to be expected. As the deficits stimulated demand for domestic goods, they also heightened demand for foreign goods. Increased imports expanded the U.S. current account deficit, which consists of the trade deficit—chiefly net imports (the negative of net exports) of goods and services—plus "unilateral transfers," gifts that Americans make to people and governments abroad (net of any reverse transfers). The current account deficit, statistical discrepancies aside, is the flip side of foreign investment in the United States; we finance the excess of our imports over our exports by running down our foreign assets or by giving foreigners greater claims on U.S. assets. This is a matter to which I shall return below in discussing the trade deficit.

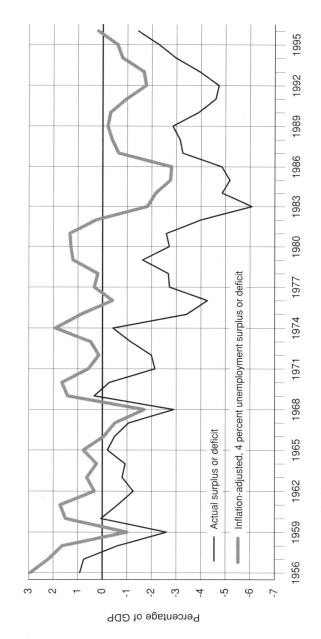

Figure 2.8. Actual and Inflation-Adjusted High-Employment Surplus or Deficit, 1956–1996 (as a percentage of GDP)

— Actual surplus or deficit

— Inflation-adjusted, 4 percent unemployment surplus or deficit

Note: The inflation-adjusted, 4 percent unemployment surplus or deficit is a result of the calculation of the "inflation tax" (the loss in real value, as measured by the change in the GDP implicit price deflator, of the average federal debt held by the public)) and a regression of differences between the actual deficit as a percentage of GDP and CBO standardized-employment deficit as a percentage of GDP on the differences between the actual unemployment rate and the CBO standardized unemployment rate based in CBO estimates of the NAIRU (non-accelerating-inflation rate of unemployment). The regression coefficient was -0.5376, indicating that each percentage point of unemployment had been associated with 0.5376 percentage points more of deficit.

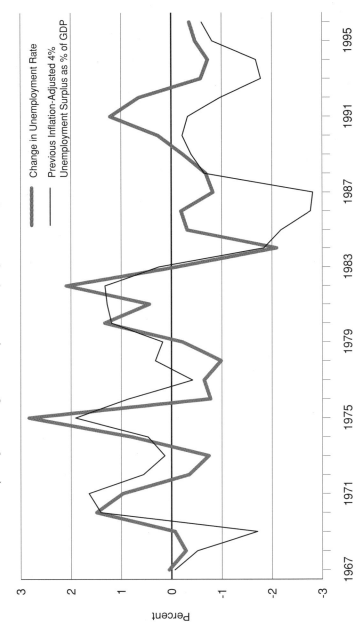

Figure 2.9. Effects of Inflation-Adjusted 4 Percent Unemployment Surplus or Deficit (as a percentage of GDP) on Unemployment Rate, 1967–1996

Note: Figure depicts change in unemployment and previous year's inflation-adjusted 4 percent unemployment surplus or deficit. The inflation-adjusted 4 percent unemployment surplus or deficit is calculated as indicated in Figure 2.8. Unemployment rates are from the *Economic Report of the President* (Washington, D.C.: Government Printing Office, 1997), Table B-33, p. 338.

There is more, however, to investment than gross private investment, domestic and foreign. There is also public investment, by federal, state, and local government, in tangible assets. There is household investment in automobiles and other consumer durables, which are not very reasonably excluded from the standard measures of gross private domestic investment. I have found each percentage point of the inflation- and cyclically adjusted deficit to be associated with about 1.1 percentage points of subsequent national saving that includes, with net foreign investment, all net investment in fixed, reproducible capital—that is, plant and equipment, houses, and all durable goods—by households or consumers as well as by business and nonprofit institutions, and all net investment in business inventories.[21]

And then there is investment in education, which is also positively related to these inflation-adjusted, high-employment deficits. Far from "crowding out" investment, then, as many argue, deficits have had the effect of crowding it in.

Two bits of further explanation are in order. First, a crude correlation of actual budget deficits with GDP, unemployment, and investment may not yield these results. That is because—and this is of the utmost importance—changes in actual deficits are to a considerable extent the outcome of changes in the economy. The Congressional Budget Office, for instance, has estimated that the short-term effect of a one percentage point reduction in the unemployment rate is a drop in the actual deficit of about $40 billion. My own estimates put it somewhat higher. Over the longer run, the deficit shrinks more as the lower debt resulting from the accumulation of lesser deficits reduces interest payments.

In terms of growth rates, a one percentage point increase in the projected rate of growth, from 2.3 percent per year to 3.3 percent, would lift output in the year 2002 by about $500 billion over what it would otherwise be. This spurt in GDP would so raise tax revenues and reduce outlays that all by itself it would lessen that year's deficit by about $150 billion. The lower interest costs on the smaller accumulated debt would diminish the deficit still further. The deficit would be completely eliminated—the budget balanced or in surplus—with no cuts in government programs or Social Security and no increase in tax rates.

Second, some economists argue that deficits must crowd out investment because government borrowing deprives private business of funds that it would use to finance investment. This ignores the fact that the government spends the funds it borrows and puts them back into circulation.[22] Budget deficits do not themselves affect the quantity or availability of money; the Federal Reserve does. Another way to confirm that deficits have no first-order effect on credit conditions is to examine the consequences of eliminating the deficit by raising taxes. It is true that the government would not then be borrowing from potential investors funds that they would otherwise lend to business. The IRS would be taking those funds instead; they would still not be available for business loans.

Related to this argument is one widely promoted by Secretary Rubin and the Clinton administration, that lower budget deficits stimulate the economy by bringing lower interest rates. This argument has been repeated so frequently that it has become a matter of faith in financial as well as political circles. Alas, economists of all persuasions have been trying for some time to find a clear relation between budget deficits and interest rates, and they have generally been unsuccessful. A stronger economy does tend to raise interest rates and a weaker economy to lower them. And the Federal Reserve seems clearly able to affect them. Indeed, the fall in interest rates that followed the adoption of Clinton's deficit reduction package early in his first administration stemmed directly from the role of the Federal Reserve. Alan Greenspan signaled this not merely in his own usually elliptical comments but by sitting between Hillary Clinton and Tipper Gore in the audience for President Clinton's first State of the Union address. There was a definite understanding that the Fed would lower interest rates if deficit reduction were put in place. But would it not have been possible to lower interest rates without a deficit reduction package? And might not that combination of monetary stimulus and fiscal neutrality—if not fiscal stimulus—have led to more growth for the economy?

So far, even after adjusting for inflation and employment, this discussion has been considering the gross budget deficit, the difference between the federal government's total outlays and total revenues. But this ignores the vital distinction between current operating expenditures and capital outlays. If corporations presented their income statements in this fashion, many if not most would be reporting losses rather than profits on their bottom line. In fact, business accounting separates out capital expenditures, recognizing that when a business purchases a machine tool or invests in a plant upgrade, it acquires an asset that will continue to produce services for years to come. Thus, the full purchase price of capital equipment is not charged against current income. Only depreciation on past investments, generally a much lower figure than current capital outlays,[23] is so charged.

Federal capital outlays, narrowly defined to include only real tangible property, have been so limited in recent years that excluding them and substituting capital consumption allowances or depreciation on past investment would not bring about a major reduction in the measured deficit. A more inclusive measure of capital expenditures, including outlays for the human capital involved in education, training, and health and other intangible capital such as research, would increase the amount of the correction and would seem more appropriate.[24]

The failure to keep a separate capital budget contributes to a faulty picture of the budget's impact on the economy and to bad economic policy. Capital of all kinds—public and private, physical and intangible, human and nonhuman—contributes to future production. If deficits add to our stock of productive capital, they actually help secure the future—for our children and grandchildren.[25] Failing to distinguish between current and capital outlays in the federal budget is to invite deficit-cutting measures that reduce public investment in the name of a better future but that actually have the opposite effect.

It has been suggested[26] that there are three views of the deficit:

1. The wolf at the door. If someone doesn't drive him away he will huff and puff and blow the house down.

2. Termites in the foundation. If they are not exterminated, the house will eventually crumble.

3. A pussycat. She will do no harm at all.

The "wolf" notion, that the sky is falling and disaster is near, is clearly nonsense. Although there have been nominal deficits for most of the past six decades, and an unbroken string now since 1970, judgment day is yet to come.

The "termites" issue is the fundamental one of whether deficits are reducing the amount of capital available for future use. Deficit "hawks" (who would cut the deficit) must use this as their argument if they are to make any economic sense. But as suggested here—and as my own work elsewhere strongly argues—growth in the real, structural deficit has increased investment and raised the amount of capital that can be bequeathed to the generations that follow.

That leaves us with the "pussycat." The damage here is more likely to come from starving her, to the detriment and anguish of most Americans. We will all be better off over the long run if she is fed a considerable diet of public investment. That will thwart any threatening termites.

- Prudent deficits, measured correctly, then, can be good for us. If they are put to good use, they can be very good for us.

- Conversely, reducing underlying structural deficits, let alone eliminating them entirely, can be harmful. It can slow the economy and even bring on a recession. It can also make it very difficult if not impossible to fund the public investment and investment in human capital so vital to our future

- Thanks in great part to the relative prosperity of the nation's robust economy, U.S. budget deficits are now the smallest by far, as a percentage of GDP, of any major country's. But take warning: Deficit paranoia and budget-balancing mania can be dangerous, extremely dangerous, to our economic health.

3

FOREIGN TRADE

Trade deficit hits record high! So read the headlines. And so what?[1]

Before hitting the panic button, one should ask, what is this talk about? Trade in what? Goods? Services? Would this encompass the services rendered by capital, that is, the earnings on investment? How about "unilateral transfers" or gifts? Including all of these is the way to approach a more meaningful "balance on current account," which corresponds in principle (except for a statistical discrepancy) to net foreign investment.

According to old mercantilist doctrine, before Adam Smith and his *Wealth of Nations* took over modern economics, a trade surplus was to be encouraged. The excess of exports over imports was rewarded in the form of gold and silver. The more of this a country had, the better off it was supposed to be. Of course, one could not eat gold and silver, and there was much hunger. But the accumulated bullion enabled a government to finance wars and hence to increase its power, for whatever that was worth.

John Maynard Keynes, undoubtedly the most influential economist of the twentieth century—and to many the greatest—pointed out in his classic *General Theory of Employment, Interest and Money* that mercantilist policies made a certain sense in an economy suffering from excess unemployment. Goods manufactured in other countries do not employ workers at home; exports of goods to other countries do. If there were no other way of putting people to work, they could be given jobs producing for other nations. The income they received from such production and foreign sales would be spent, to a large extent, at home. That would stimulate additional production to satisfy this export-induced demand, in accordance with what is known as a "multiplier effect" (in this case an international trade multiplier). An increase of $1 billion in exports might put fifty thousand people to work. These fifty thousand would buy another billion dollars worth of goods, putting another fifty thousand to work. Total national income and output would then increase by $2 billion.

The attempt to achieve export surpluses became an important part of efforts to combat the rising unemployment of the Great Depression of the 1930s. It was, though, a "zero-sum" game. Clearly, for the world as a whole, exports must equal imports.[2] One country's trade surplus was therefore another's—or some combination of others'—trade deficit. The policy was aptly labeled one of "beggar-my-neighbor." Each country tried to export its unemployment to another nation. The main means of accomplishing this was restricting imports, generally by high tariffs. What was not spent on imports, it was presumed, would be spent on domestic goods, providing domestic employment that would be supplemented by the jobs of those producing for export.

But as all countries tried to play this game, they became worse off. Aside from the general loss of efficiency as each nation failed to capitalize on its comparative advantage and specialize in the production to which it was best suited, every nation's restrictions on imports[3] reduced the exports of others. World trade shrank, to the detriment of all.

To this day, though, nations seem obsessed with encouraging their exports and, where they can, developing trade surpluses. These have certainly contributed to employment and profits in the exporting industries. Whether they have proved to be optimal long-run policies is questionable. Providing jobs and profits through production for domestic needs might, after all, have done more for the lasting prosperity and growth of nations that have relied on export surpluses, Japan being the outstanding example.

Trade deficits, however, absent full employment, are considered damaging. The U.S. automobile industry decries American purchases of Japanese cars. (Boeing, of course, welcomes purchases of our planes throughout Asia and the world.) But is it really necessary to give up buying Toyotas, whether made in Japan or Kentucky, to combat unemployment? Do Americans have to sacrifice the inexpensive clothing and electronics that contribute to our very large trade deficit with China?

The nature of trade is changing. Goods or merchandise trade, while still the largest component by far in the nation's total current account, are almost matched by the total of trade in services and investment income. While the United States has been running a large deficit in goods—$188 billion in 1996—it has been running a surplus in services, so that the deficit in goods and services combined was a considerably smaller $114 billion in that same year. The United States is by far the world's greatest exporter of services, with its total reaching $223.9 billion in 1996, compared with $150.4 billion in imports. This imbalance may well grow as trade barriers come down in the booming industries of information technology, telecommunications, and financial services, in all of which the United States is particularly strong.

Net investment income—the difference between receipts from U.S. assets abroad and payments on foreign assets held in the United States—was substantially positive for many years, reaching a peak of almost $24 billion in 1990, but it fell to only $3 billion in 1996. The fall reflected a drop in the net international investment position of the United States by the beginning of 1996 to a negative $774 billion. Many years of U.S. current account deficits added to net foreign assets in the United States. Since the beginning of 1988, foreign investment in the United States has increased by almost $2.5 trillion—about $700 billion of this invested directly in factories, hotels, and the like, and the rest in financial instruments such as Treasury securities, corporate stocks and bonds, and assets in U.S. banks. Total U.S. assets abroad, by contrast, have risen by only a little more than $1.6 trillion during the same period. U.S. net investment income was still positive, if only slightly so, in 1996 because American investors enjoy a considerably higher rate of return on their assets in the rest of the world than foreigners do on their greater investments in the United States.

Also contributing to the current account deficit, the United States "gives" to the rest of the world more—$42 billion more in 1996—than it gets in the form of unilateral transfers. These include individual gifts by American residents to relatives in the "old country," Social

Security payments to former American residents who returned to their countries of origin for their retirement years, and some of Washington's considerably reduced foreign aid.

All this adds up to a negative "balance on current account" of $165 billion in 1996—about the same as the deficit of $167 billion in 1987, when U.S. GDP was more than a third smaller. In 1996 the current account deficit was 2.18 percent of GDP; in 1987 it was 3.57 percent. But whatever the numbers, what do they mean?

The deficit on current account signifies that the amount that Americans are receiving from other countries exceeds what they are sending abroad. Aside from the employment problem, one might conclude that the more the United States gets from foreigners the better. They do all the work producing those Japanese automobiles and Chinese shirts, and we get to drive the cars and wear the clothing. We are in this sense better off for sustaining the trade and current account deficits.

The catch is that this current account deficit is matched—and must be matched, since unilateral transfers have already been taken into account—by an increase in what has incorrectly been called our net debt to foreigners. Indeed, in the 1988 election campaign, and frequently since, it has been lamented that the United States has become the "world's greatest debtor nation." This statement was in no sense true in 1988, and its meaning is dubious today.

What is true is that when the United States has a current account deficit we are "buying" more from foreigners than they are buying from us. Foreigners thus generally acquire more dollars than they give up.[4] These dollars then constitute foreign claims on U.S. assets. Foreigners can keep these claims in American or other banks or, more likely, use them to buy anything from U.S. Treasury bills to stocks in American companies, from Rockefeller Center to another Toyota factory in Kentucky.

"The net international investment position of the United States," as it is called, however, depends on more than the accumulation of these assets or claims year by year. It also depends—or should depend, if measured right—on changes in the value of these claims. This depends on both fluctuations in the local-currency value of assets and liabilities and movements in exchange rates; that is, what foreign currencies are worth in U.S. dollars. The original assertion that the United States had become the "world's greatest debtor nation" ignored many of these changes in value, particularly for direct investment in manufacturing plant and other assets.

Taking into account the variations in value makes a big difference.[5] American investments in the rest of the world were undertaken in large part many years ago and have increased enormously in value. Foreign investments in the United States have been more recent and, at least by 1988, had not appreciated nearly as much. Correcting for the changes in asset values, using an adjustment based either on current costs or changes in stock market prices, would have wiped out most of our $800 billion negative balance at that time. Since then, however, continued deficits on current account and the renewed appreciation of the dollar, which reduces the dollar value of U.S. foreign assets, have put the U.S. international investment position back in the red. By the end of 1996, it was a negative $871 billion, measuring direct investment at current cost, and a negative $831 billion when measured at market values.

There are still other corrections that make a difference. One relates to immigration to the United States. The holdings of all residents of the United States are properly deemed U.S. assets, wherever they are located. Thus, when rich South Americans decide to settle in Miami, or rich Japanese in Hawaii, all of their assets, whether in their country of origin, in the United States, in Switzerland or some other third country, should be counted as a gain in U.S. assets—an increase in U.S. claims on the rest of the world or a decrease in foreign claims on U.S. assets. In fact, such gains in U.S. net claims are rarely picked up in the official accounts kept by the Bureau of Economic Analysis. There is an associated general problem, of unknown dimension, of secret or anonymous bank accounts kept abroad by U.S. residents; these may contribute to the substantial statistical discrepancy, or "errors and omissions," in the official accounts.

Assume that the current account deficit of some $165 billion, or even its 2.17916 percent of GDP, will remain constant indefinitely. This does not mean that the United States, in a meaningful, relative sense, will fall further and further into debt. For one thing, the resulting net foreign investment in the United States is largely not in the form of debt—that is, in fixed monetary obligations—but in equity or other assets offering no concrete claims in earnings or capital values. For another, as in the case of the budget deficit and the domestic debt-to-GDP ratio, the ratio of net foreign claims to GDP will over time approach the ratio of the current account deficit to the rate of growth in GDP. Again, assuming a 5 percent annual rate of growth of nominal GDP, this means that even with a continuing current account deficit beginning at its 1996 level and growing 5 percent per year, net foreign claims would, as a ratio of GDP, rise to but never exceed 43.58311 percent, as illustrated in Figure 3.1.

Lest that seem worrisome, consider the likely cost of servicing such obligations. With a real rate of return at a relatively high 4 percent, the United States would be paying the rest of the world all of 1.74 percent of its GDP each year. How much this would cost would depend on what the rest of the world does with this return. If foreigners merely allow it to accumulate in more investments in the United States, it does not really cost us anything. If they use it to buy American goods and services in a full-employment economy, they necessarily consume goods and services that would otherwise be available to Americans. But at the same time they reduce or eliminate the deficit on current account, so that the ratio of net foreign claims to GDP declines. If unemployment is a problem in this country, the choice of the rest of the world to use its earnings to buy more U.S. goods and services will put more Americans to work.

There may be good reason to believe that foreigners will be content to continue accumulating American assets. The United States is, after all, a pretty safe and promising haven for investors. The desire of the rest of the world to hold U.S. assets—and to hold increasing amounts of U.S. assets as the growth of their own economies gives them more to invest—may well be a major contributor to maintaining the value of the dollar. This, in turn, generates a demand for foreign goods and services, which become cheaper to Americans with a more valuable dollar, and adds to the trade and current account deficits that give foreigners the dollars they want to accumulate. Americans may in effect be getting a free ride—or free lunch—from foreigners who are willing to exchange their goods and services for dollar assets they may never cash in.

But what if they do decide to cash in? There are frequent warnings about skating on dangerous ice. For want of domestic saving, it is said, investment in the United States is being financed by foreigners. Suppose the Japanese finally signal that they are tired of accumulating dollar assets. They decide to throw in the towel, as they did with Rockefeller Center, and take their dollars and convert them to yen. Who has yen to give them? Obviously, other Japanese! But if other Japanese give up yen in return for dollars, the Japanese have not pulled out at all! (And if the Japanese convert their dollars to other currencies, say German marks, then it is the Germans who

**Figure 3.1. Net Foreign Claims, If Current Account Deficit Remains at
1996 Level and GDP Increases at 5 Percent Per Year, 1996–2200
(as percentage of GDP)**

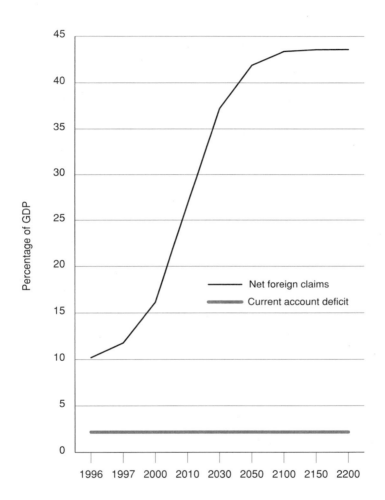

Source: Initial figures from the *Survey of Current Business* (March 1997), D-61, Table
G-I, "International Investment at Year-End, 1994 and 1995." Author's projections
assume constant current account deficit at 1996's 2.18 percentage of GDP.

are holding dollar assets; there has been no aggregate pullout by foreigners.)

What does happen is that the effort to sell dollars for yen drives down the value of the dollar. As the dollar becomes cheaper, Americans find foreign goods and services more expensive, and foreigners get better bargains from the United States. The result is that the U.S. trade deficit and current account deficit are reduced. If the latter switches to a surplus, then and only then do foreigners pull out—that is, lessen their net claims on the United States. They can pull out only by taking our goods and services—or making us a gift of their assets.

In general, excesses in the current account deficit or in foreign claims will be corrected, sooner or later, by changes in exchange rates. Declines in the value of the dollar will eventually reduce or even reverse the current account deficit and the increase in net foreign claims. I say "eventually" because of the well-known "S-Curve" short-term response of trade to a fall in the exchange rate (see Figure 3.2). It has been found that drops in the exchange rate frequently tend initially to increase the trade deficit—driving the trade balance further down on the sideways "S" shown in the figure.

This occurs in part because people are slow to change their buying habits and do not immediately purchase fewer foreign goods as they become more expensive. Producers also may be slow to take advantage of new export opportunities as foreigners become more willing customers. Eventually, however, the inevitable law of supply and demand takes hold. Other things being equal, people do buy more of goods that become cheaper and less of those that become expensive. The trade balance changes direction, moving up that horizontal "S" curve and approaching a new equilibrium, shown optimistically in the illustrative figure to be at a zero deficit.

What if economists' confidence in their basic law of supply and demand proves misplaced? Suppose misguided government policy leads Washington to borrow excessively abroad. Might this not bring on a crisis such as the recent one in Mexico or other debt crises that have led to default or the need for costly international bailouts? This is, fortunately, not a worry for the United States. Foreign claims on this country are almost exclusively in dollars. Most of them, as noted, are not even fixed claims on money or bonds. The "foreign and international" claims in the form of holdings of the federal debt came to $1,131 billion[6] at the end of the fourth quarter of 1996, some 29 percent of the gross federal debt held by the public. The amount held as

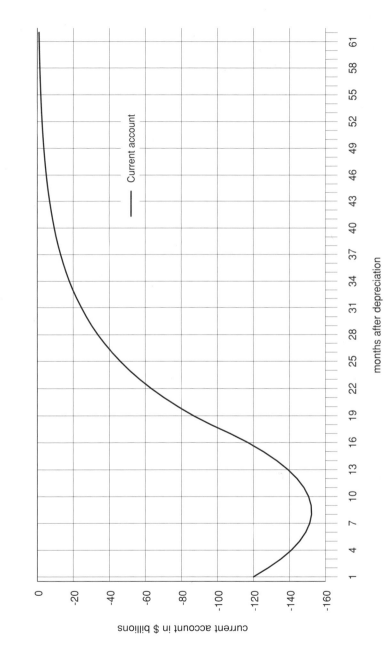

Figure 3.2. Hypothetical S-Curve Response of the Current Account to a Depreciation of a Nation's Currency ($ billions)

debt depends not so much on the total of gross foreign assets in the United States—$5,116 billion with direct investment measured at market value at the end of 1996[7]—as on the portfolio choices of foreigners, including foreign central banks that are likely to invest in U.S. Treasury securities.

If foreigners try to "collect" on any of their claims, they only lower the value of the dollar in regard to their own currency and take a beating. The United States does incur some losses in deteriorating terms of trade, having to pay more for foreign goods and to sell more American products in exchange. But these effects are of second order, given the size of the American economy.[8] In the last analysis, if foreigners want to collect in dollars, U.S. monetary authorities can create all the dollars they want, actually printing them if citizens are willing to endure the inflation that would cause or, in the usual ways of modern banking, having the Federal Reserve create them by its open-market purchases.

Americans therefore have little to fear from deficits in trade or the more inclusive (and relevant) current account, so long as these do not threaten domestic employment. There is no gainsaying, however, that trade can threaten particular industries and their workers. Cheap Chinese clothing is a boon to the American consumer but may be a disaster to workers in the U.S. apparel industry. Japanese carmakers may force U.S. manufacturers to compete by holding down wages or "downsizing." Car buyers benefit from lower costs, whether for domestic or foreign vehicles, and higher quality. But American workers in the automotive industry are on balance worse off.

The law of comparative advantage says that free trade will encourage each nation to specialize in production for which it has a relative advantage (which could mean a lesser disadvantage). The American airliner industry is doing very well. But the comfort of Boeing employees in Seattle does not ease the discomfort of those who have lost their jobs or relatively high wages in Detroit. The truth is that there will always be groups of people that are adversely affected by change in free markets. In order to reduce pressures to curtail free trade, it is important that the government take measures to ease the transitions as rapidly changing world markets produce losers as well as gainers. Training and retraining, improvements in labor markets, increases in labor mobility, and subsidies for hiring displaced workers may well be in order.

Efforts to protect particular industries and their workers by restricting imports, however, are destined to prove counterproductive for the economy as a whole. The problem is not merely that the Japanese, for instance, may retaliate by further restricting imports of American products, although they might well do so, or at least stiffen resistance to efforts to open up their markets. There is, rather, a boomerang effect to be expected in completely free markets. If the United States applies quotas or tariffs or other restrictive measures that reduce imports, it supplies fewer dollars to the rest of the world. The laws of supply and demand apply as much to dollars as to peanuts. A more expensive dollar resulting from a shrinking supply means that prospective buyers will find Boeing planes relatively more expensive than Airbus planes made in Europe. The jobs that may be saved in Detroit may be lost in Seattle.

When there are trade deficits, though, those landing jobs producing for export are outnumbered by those losing them because imports are supplanting domestic production. And this is aggravated at times when the economy is not at full employment. Government policies to achieve as full a measure of employment as possible thus become essential.

One tool for increasing employment is to drive interest rates as low as possible, and certainly to do nothing to prevent them from falling to wherever a free market will take them. Lower interest rates tend generally to increase investment of all kinds, putting people to work producing new houses, business plant and equipment, and public infrastructure financed by borrowing. Increased investment not only enhances current prosperity but provides more real capital to live on in the future.

Lower interest rates also lower the international demand for the dollar and hence reduce its exchange rate. This will tend to increase U.S. exports and reduce imports. Certain costs will increase as our terms of trade deteriorate, but smaller trade and current account deficits, to the extent that these result once the Federal Reserve is no longer pursuing tight money policies, will be the dividend of the more efficient division of production between the United States and the rest of the world. (To the other costs of the "peremptory strikes" by the Fed that raise interest rates to combat inflation when there are no visible signs of price pressures should be added the costs of contrived deficits in the U.S. balance of payments.)

It is sometimes argued that our current account deficit and the accompanying foreign investment in the United States are depriving the investing countries and others, in particular less-developed nations, of much-needed capital. Reducing this deficit is not likely, however, to make more capital available elsewhere. If Americans reduce purchases of goods and services from the rest of the world or sell more to it, they simply reduce the net supply of dollars to other nations. These will be investing less in the United States because they will have fewer dollars to work with. There will be still less to invest elsewhere. It is true that if Americans do not purchase as much from other developed countries more of their resources will be free to produce goods for the rest of the world. But that will not in itself give less-developed countries the foreign currency or credit that would enable them to acquire these goods. Also, it may be observed that current account surpluses did not prevent developing countries such as China and Mexico from receiving huge amounts of private direct investment in 1996—in the case of China, $73.3 billion despite a particularly large overall surplus.[9]

There is, it should be warned, one utterly abhorrent way to reduce U.S. deficits with the rest of the world. That would be to slow our own economy. In a recession, Americans would buy less of everything, foreign as well as domestic. The reduction in imports would pare or even eliminate the trade deficit, but at a high price in terms of lost domestic production overall and lower employment.

Deficits also fluctuate with economic conditions abroad. Greater prosperity and growth in other nations will increase their purchases from the United States and reduce this country's deficits. This kind of deficit reduction is all to the good. Americans should welcome the good fortune of others and do what can be done to further it.

U.S. policy, then, should strive for full employment and the most productive domestic economy possible. It should avoid monetary prescriptions that produce high interest rates and an overvalued dollar. Policymakers should indeed discourage other nations from overvaluing the dollar. If the Bank of Japan persists in buying dollars to keep the currency's value high and thus artificially to encourage Japanese exports, American leaders might be prepared to suggest that two can play that game: the Federal Reserve can readily buy yen with newly created dollars.

While a central bank such as the Federal Reserve may not be able to defy market forces for long and prop up or raise the price of an overvalued currency, it can lower the value of its currency if it is determined to do so. This asymmetry owes to the fact that in order to keep up the value of its currency a central bank has to be able to offer foreign exchange at the existing price to all who want to sell its currency. But a central bank's holdings of assets denominated in the currency of other nations are limited. Further, as investors or speculators sense that the bank may run out of foreign exchange and be unable to maintain the value of its currency, they rush to sell that currency, anticipating (often correctly) that when its price does indeed fall they will be able to buy it back at a considerable profit.

But to lower the price of its currency, a central bank need only use its own money to buy other currencies. Since a central bank is the ultimate creator of money, it can buy foreign currencies indefinitely, deterred only by the concern that it will be inflating its own money supply and quite possibly its economy as well. I would guess, though, that if the Federal Reserve battled with the Bank of Japan over which could more effectively hold down the value of its currency vis-a-vis the other's, the Japanese would cry "uncle" before the inflationary concern became prohibitive.

But if exchange rates are free to play their ultimately equilibrating role, and if government follows appropriate fiscal and monetary policies at home to achieve maximum employment, Americans have nothing to fear from trade deficits, deficits in the current account, or net foreign investment in the United States. Like the concerns about budget deficits, such fears are illusory. Moreover, efforts to eliminate these deficits can prove very costly, whether they entail interfering with the efficiencies to be gained from trade or curbing our own economy.

4

SOCIAL SECURITY[1]

The myths about Social Security are perhaps the worst of all the deficit scare stories. They frighten millions of elderly and millions more who hope someday to be elderly. They offer cover for insidious efforts to diminish or destroy a system of social insurance that has served its purpose well for six decades.

It is said that the Social Security trust funds are in prospective deficit, projected to become insolvent in about thirty years, so there will be no "money" to pay retirees. This is nonsense. Aside from the notorious inaccuracy of long-run (and other) projections, money can always be put into the trust funds by a simple act of Congress.

Some assert that the federal government is "masking" the true budget deficit by spending workers' contributions to the trust funds and giving the funds in return worthless paper in the form of non-negotiable Treasury securities. Also nonsense! The budget deficit, as pointed out earlier, is the excess of total outlays by the Treasury over total revenues. All "contributions for social insurance" go directly to the Treasury, and Social Security checks—as retirees can readily attest—come directly from the Treasury. And if Treasury securities or promises by the government to pay are worthless, then so is all our money.

Public opinion polls yield cynical responses from a majority of respondents that Social Security benefits will not "be there for them." That will occur only if Congress defaults or if the economy so breaks down that the real goods and services these benefits would buy are not available in any case. My sense is there will always be enough voting elderly, along with their concerned children, to block congressional default. And only an extreme gloom-and-doomer can honestly expect an utter collapse of our economy.

There is one real deficit in Social Security. That is the shortfall in what is necessary to ensure that all Americans enjoy in their golden years at least the standard of living they enjoyed when they were younger. Our retirement system should indeed go further and enable the elderly to share in the advances of a growing economy.

Social Security deficits have been dramatized in two ways. The first, which makes no economic sense, is that the system is somehow on the verge of bankruptcy or will at some time in the future be unable to finance promised benefits. The second, which has some legitimacy but whose import is grossly exaggerated, is that the aging of our population will leave so many elderly relative to those working that the state will be short of the resources necessary to support them. Consider, then, these two issues: 1) the use and financing of the Old Age and Survivors and Disability Insurance trust funds (OASDI); and 2) the real support of those not employed—the dependent population, young and old—by those working.

The problem with the OASDI trust funds, if there is one, is utterly trivial. Many people talk as if these "funds" contained piles of $100 bills, which workers replenish with their contributions. At the risk of causing more worry, I must point out that there is no "money" in the trust funds; their assets are Treasury obligations, as good as money but essentially computer entries, printed out each month. These indicate what the Treasury has credited the funds: to correspond to payroll taxes; to meet the interest payments that the Treasury, in conformity with current law, awards the funds on their computer balances; and to figure in a minor amount from proceeds of the taxation of benefits.

Since Social Security checks come from the Treasury in any event, there is no real reason to go through the accounting procedure of building up the computer balances and then drawing them down. The funds could be abolished and the Treasury ordered to go on paying the benefits prescribed by law, borrowing to finance these expenditures if necessary, just as it does now to finance the U.S. military or anything else. Payroll taxes, like other taxes, go into the general Treasury pot that finances expenditures, and dropping a separate account for them would make no difference. To the argument that retirees would be less secure without the funds, it should be emphasized again that the integrity of commitments to the elderly depends ultimately on the political will to meet them and the nation's real economic ability to do so. Neither of these should be in doubt.

As to the alleged future insolvency of the funds, this concern stems from what are known as the "intermediate" long-run projections of the funds' trustees and their actuaries and economists. The funds also issue "high-cost" projections that forecast insolvency sooner and "low-cost" projections, which foretell no solvency problem whatsoever. The intermediate projections now indicate that by the year 2029 the funds' assets, which will have grown enormously in the intervening years, reaching $2.89 trillion in 2018,[2] will be exhausted, and current receipts at that time will cover only about three-quarters of anticipated annual expenditures.[3] What most alarmists fail to mention is the observation, in the trustees' report, that an increase in taxes of a mere 2.23 percent of taxable payroll would, by these intermediate projections, keep the funds fully solvent through the year 2070.

Besides, there are many feasible solutions that require no increase in taxes. For one, policymakers could simply credit the funds with: a) the income taxes now paid as a result of certain Social Security payroll "contributions" not being deductible in computing taxable incomes, and b) higher interest returns on the fund balances. The nondeductible Social Security contributions include all payroll taxes on employees and half of the taxes paid by the self-employed. Their total now runs about $200 billion a year. With income tax rates averaging about 17 percent, crediting the trust funds with the income taxes paid on the nondeductible Social Security contributions would give them an additional $35 billion this year, about half of the 2.23 percent of taxable payroll that the intermediate projections indicate would be adequate for long-term solvency. Crediting the funds with returns on their asset balances three percentage points more than under current law—about 9.3 percent instead of a projected 6.3 percent—would easily make up the rest of the gap. This entails no change in taxes paid or government borrowing. It is indeed only an accounting maneuver, but the presumed problem with the trust funds is only an accounting problem to begin with and therefore appropriately solved by changing the paperwork.

The Treasury is already contributing out of general revenues to Medicare—$65 billion in 1996 to Medicare's Part B, the Supplementary

Medical Insurance (SMI) program.[4] Allocating other revenues to OASDI, the retirement and disability funds, thus would not establish a new precedent. Crediting to the Social Security trust funds that part of income taxes levied on payroll contributions is entirely reasonable and would make no difference whatsoever to government financing, the taxpayer, or the economy. The Treasury, after all, would be collecting these taxes as before and spending the revenue as before. Instead of the taxes going into a general funds account, however, they would be credited to the OASDI account. And those worried about the funds' solvency might breathe easier.

Crediting the fund balances with higher returns is also amply justified. It would bring them closer in level to the market equity return that advocates of privatizing some or all of the Social Security system promise. Payroll contributions to the funds have saved the Treasury from public borrowing that would have substituted for private investment. Private investors whose funds would otherwise have purchased Treasury securities thus put their money into the higher-yield stock market. It is only appropriate that Social Security participants, who cannot invest their involuntary "contributions," have their funds credited with the higher returns to private investors that these contributions have made possible. Again, this additional credit to the funds would make no difference of any real magnitude; as the "debt" of one part of the government to another, it would not even add to the relevant figure for the federal debt, which is the gross federal debt held by the public, currently $3.8 trillion.

I shall suggest another accounting change that would take care of the trust funds. Instead of restricting the funds' revenues to payroll taxes, one might also credit the funds with some of taxpayers' individual and corporate income taxes. About 1.5 percent of taxable individual and corporate income would be equivalent to the 2.23 percent increase in payroll taxes the fund trustees have calculated.

It should be stressed that none of these accounting changes affect in any real way the federal deficit or anything else. The deficit is still the excess of total government outlays over revenues. Crediting more of those receipts to a particular account—or setting up new internal accounts altogether—just juggles the surpluses and deficits within those accounts.

Not often noticed are the fund trustees' "low-cost" projections. These differ from the somber intermediate projections (and of course all the more so from the gloom-and-doom "high-cost" projections) presented with them in Figure 4.1, partly in assuming a long-run unemployment rate of 5 percent (still above the August rate of 4.9 percent), instead

Figure 4.1. When Will the Social Security Trust Funds Run Out?

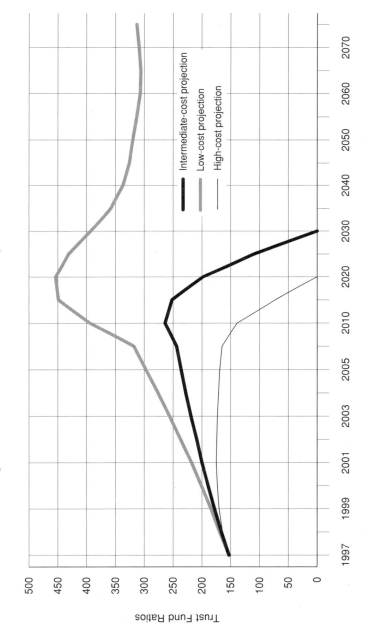

Note: The Trust Fund Ratio consists of assets at the beginning of the year, including advance tax transfers (if any), expressed as a percentage of outlays during the year.

Source: 1996 Annual Report of the Board of Trustees of the Federal Old-Age Survivors Insurance and Disability Insurance Trust Funds (Washington,D.C.: Government Printing Office, 1997), Table 1.3. 1997 Figure II F6 (Table II F20).

of the intermediate projections' 6 percent, and in projecting a twenty-first-century annual rate of growth in real GDP of about 2.2 percent—it was 2.8 percent in 1996—instead of rates of 1.3 to 1.4 percent. The low-cost projections peg Consumer Price Index inflation at 2.5 percent—closer to its current rate and average over the past several years—instead of 3.5 percent. And they also assume higher fertility and mortality rates and greater immigration. According to the low-cost projections, fund balances reach a high in 2018 of 457 percent of annual expenditures before falling to about three times annual expenditures in 2065.[5] Thereafter, they mount indefinitely. If even some of the more optimistic assumptions underlying the low-cost projections are realized, the fund will remain solvent indefinitely.

The only meaningful problem that could befall Social Security relates to the size of the working population producing the goods and services required by those who are not in the labor force. In this regard warning is given that while there are now almost five people of working age—twenty to sixty-four—for every potential dependent aged sixty-five and over, by the year 2030 that ratio will fall to less than three.

The relevant numbers, though, relate to all potential dependents, the young—under twenty years of age—as well as the old. In 1995, for every 1,000 people of working age there were 710 young and old potential dependents. In the year 2030, the intermediate projection puts the number at 788.[6] This means that those 1,000 people of working age would have to support 1,788 people—themselves and their dependents—instead of 1,710, a 4.56 percent increase in their burden.

But if productivity per worker grows at a modest 1 percent per year, well within the range of historical experience, the growth in total output per worker will exceed 40 percent by the year 2030. This would increase income per capita by more than a third, ample to improve vastly the lot of all—the elderly, the young, and those in their working prime.

An increase in the dependency ratio for the aged—putting aside for the moment a decrease in the under-twenty dependency ratio—will require those in the twenty-to-sixty-four age group, presumably the working population, to devote a greater share of their increasing incomes to supporting those sixty-five and over. But this support must be current. While people can save and invest now in more ovens that will be useful at a future time, the bread dependents eat at any time must be baked by those working then. Retirees cannot eat balances in Social Security trust funds, or stocks and bonds, or cash. In a real sense, for the economy as a whole, retirement benefits are always supplied on a pay-as-you-go basis.

That is why it makes perfect sense to finance Social Security on a pay-as-you-go basis, raising taxes on the working population to finance benefits for the expanding proportions of the aged as those increases occur. But then it must be recognized that this aging of the population about which there has been so much comment is still much in the future. The dependency ratio for the aged, at 21.4 percent in 1995, will, according to the intermediate forecast of the Social Security fund trustees, actually decline to 21.1 percent in 2000 and to 20.7 percent in 2005 before finally returning to 21.4 percent in 2010. There is hence no need whatsoever to raise taxes or cut benefits to the elderly over the next thirteen years. If there is a problem with rising dependency ratios, it is not a short-run or even an intermediate-run problem.

What share of swelling incomes and output must go to support the greater numbers of elderly when the proportions do increase— assuming it is desirable to maintain both the working and the elderly populations in the same relative position? With a dependency ratio for the elderly of 0.214 in 1995, each 1,000 people of working age must support 1,214—themselves and 214 elderly. If the dependency ratio rises to 0.239 in the year 2015, as is forecast, each 1,000 people of working age will have to support 1,239 people. Their burden will have increased by roughly 2 percent. It follows, then, that the per capita incomes of both the working population and the elderly will have to be reduced by 2 percent from what they would have been if the dependency ratio for the elderly had not risen. For the working population, this may be accomplished by increasing their taxes by 2 percent of their incomes; for the elderly, government may cut retirement benefits or, preferably, in order to keep matters fully symmetrical, increase their taxes as well by 2 percent of their incomes.

By the year 2020, when the dependency ratio for the aged is up to 0.275 and the total burden per 1,000 workers reaches 1,275, 4.98 percent above the burden in 1995, net incomes per capita of the working population and the elderly will then have to be 4.7 percent less than they would have been without the increase in the dependency ratio as shown in Table 4.1 (see page 50).[7] In 2025, net incomes will have to be 7.9 percent less. In 2030, the year of the alleged apocalypse when the trust funds will no longer be able to finance all currently legislated benefits, net incomes will have to be 10.4 percent less. If the intermediate forecasts are correct, by 2075, seventy-eight years from now, net incomes per capita will have to be 14.2 percent less.

But these cuts in net income per capita are all relative. If the average income per worker increases at even a very modest 1 percent a year, the Social Security-related reductions in net income per capita will still leave everybody—the young, the working population, and the aged—with higher absolute incomes, far better off than today. In 2030, per capita income would be 26.9 percent more, and in 2075 it would be 90.2 percent more, as Table 4.1 clearly shows.

Leading newspapers, including the *New York Times* (in a March 1 editorial) and the *Wall Street Journal* (a March 6 editorial), along with economists such as former Reagan Council of Economic Advisers chairman Martin Feldstein (in the February 26 *Wall Street Journal*) and Federal Reserve Chairman Alan Greenspan, have urged balancing the federal budget by applying new, lower measures of inflation. This would reduce Social Security benefits from what they would otherwise be; in truth, would reduce them much more

Table 4.1. Changes in Dependency Ratios for the Aged and Net Incomes Per Capita

Year	Dependency ratio* for the aged	Burden per worker (1 + dependency ratio) as percentage of 1995	Percentage change in net income per capita because of increase in dependency ratio	Percentage increase in net income per worker from 1 % per annum growth	Percentage net change in income
1995	0.214	100.0	0.0	0.0	0.0
2000	0.211	99.8	+0.2	5.1	+5.4
2005	0.207	99.4	+0.5	10.5	+11.0
2010	0.214	100.0	0.0	16.1	+16.1
2015	0.239	102.05	-2.0	22.0	+19.6
2020	0.275	104.98	-4.7	28.2	+22.2
2025	0.319	108.61	-7.9	34.8	+24.1
2030	0.355	111.61	-10.4	41.7	+26.9
2075	0.415	116.56	-14.2	121.7	+90.2

* From *1997 Annual Report of the Board of Trustees of the Federal Old-Age and Survivors Insurance and Disability Insurance Trust Funds* (Washington, D.C.: Government Printing Office, 1997), Table II.H1, p. 148.

substantially than generally acknowledged. A downward adjustment of 1.1 percent in the inflation rate measured by the consumer price index—as recommended by the commission authorized by the Senate Finance Committee and chaired by Michael Boskin, chairman of the Council of Economic Advisers under President Bush—"sounded all right" to the *Journal* and others.

While 1.1 percent sounds like a small amount, such a cut would have a large effect on Social Security benefits and the retirement income of most Americans. Social Security and many private retirement plans are adjusted for inflation. Assume the rate of inflation as measured by the current CPI is 2.2 percent, the actual increase recorded from May 1996 to May 1997. With an annual "cost-of-living" adjustment of 2.2 percent, the average retiree would see benefits increase in nominal dollars by 55 percent in about twenty years, the average period of time in which a retiree receives benefits. If adjustments were tied to a CPI increasing by only 1.1 percent, the increase in nominal benefits would amount to only 24 percent.

Average Social Security benefits for a family with a retired worker now total about $10,000.[8] With the smaller adjustment, benefits that begin at $10,000 would come to $12,446 at the end of twenty years instead of $15,453—a reduction of 19.5 percent. Since the average household with a retiree receives some 62 percent of its income from Social Security, its total income would be about 12 percent less when the last check comes in and about 5 or 6 percent less over the entire period in which it receives benefits.

The bottom fifth of Social Security households receive less than $6,000 a year, and that constitutes 81 percent of their income on average. It would mean cutting these recipients' total income by 15.7 percent by the end of their lives, and by an average of about 7 percent over their entire benefit period. Do we really want to do that to these elderly poor, whose total income would otherwise average all of $7,500 over the period they would be receiving benefits? And should benefits to middle-income retirees really be cut? Consider that pensioners' average total income, which currently amounts to some $16,000, would be sliced by 5 or 6 percent.

Something of a myth has developed that the elderly are generally well-off—too well-off. There are, of course, some wealthy elderly, just as there are wealthy youngsters like Bill Gates and Michael Eisner. But, as pointed out in a Public Policy Institute fact sheet drawing on the Census Bureau's March 1996 *Current Population Survey*, the median income in 1995 of households with members sixty-five and over was $19,096, compared with a median for all households of $34,076. The percentage of persons below the official poverty rate in 1995 was 10.5 percent for those sixty-five and over, and it was also greater than 10 percent for those from fifty-five to sixty-four, while it was 9.4 percent and 7.8 percent, respectively, for those aged thirty-five to forty-four and forty-five to fifty-four. If the definition of "poor" is extended to those with incomes less than 25 percent above the poverty level, the 17.7 percent figure for the sixty-five-and-over group is higher than that of any group above twenty-five years of age.[9] Much larger proportions of children and youths live in poverty or close to it, but that is a scandal in itself (see Figure 4.2).

Daniel Radner of the Social Security Administration has compiled and adjusted for family size and number of children measures of "comprehensive income" that include food stamps, school lunches, housing subsidies, and the earned income tax credit net of taxes.[10] These calculations indicate still-greater proportions of elderly poor, both absolutely and relatively. In 1994, for example, 11.7 percent of those sixty-five and over were reported to fall below the official poverty level, but 15.6 percent could have been classified as poor for having adjusted incomes less than half of the national median. Less than 12 percent of those between the ages of thirty-five and fifty-nine fell into this expanded category of the poor.

The situation is much worse for many older women living alone. The mean private pension for older women, as pointed out in a recent Twentieth Century Fund publication,[11] yields $3,940 annually, compared to $7,468 for men; and 37 percent of older women living alone rely on their generally smaller Social Security checks for at least 90 percent of their income.

What finally determines Social Security benefits should not be what one formula or another for adjusting the CPI yields but rather what is fair. What is fair to the elderly and to their children and grandchildren who are supporting them in this, the world's wealthiest and most successful economy, an economy that is still growing and can be expected to grow, perhaps more rapidly, in the future? The current formula's results hardly indicate that the elderly are being treated too well. Most have little or nothing in the way of accumulated savings or wealth to supplement their often inadequate incomes.

"Correcting" the cost-of-living adjustment, no matter what standard is used, would condemn retirees to static real incomes while those

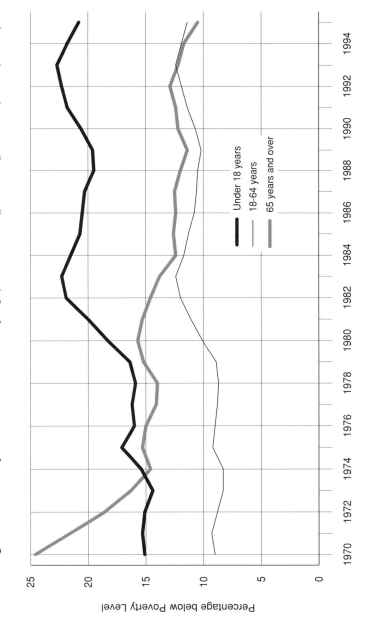

Figure 4.2. Poverty Status of Americans by Age, 1970–1995 (percentage below poverty level)

Under 18 years
18-64 years
65 years and over

Percentage below Poverty Level

1970 1972 1974 1976 1978 1980 1982 1984 1986 1988 1990 1992 1994

Source: Eleanor Baugher and Leatha Lamison-White, U.S. Department of Commerce, Bureau of the Census, *Current Population Reports* Series P60-194, *Poverty in the United States: 1995* (Washington, D.C.: U.S. Government Printing Office, 1995), Table C-2.

of the young grew with the increasing productivity of the economy. Public opinion polls indicate an overwhelming sentiment among those of all ages that Social Security benefits should be increased, not reduced. One step in the right direction would be to adjust benefits after retirement to changes in wages rather than to any measure of the CPI. This would enable the elderly to continue to share in the progress of the economy instead of falling further and further behind their juniors.

Other proposals are afoot to *cut* Social Security benefits. Extending the "normal" retirement age is particularly insidious because it has little to do with inducing workers to retire later. It would, rather, reduce benefits whenever they retire. Currently, benefits are scaled back for those who retire early, say at sixty-two, and increased for those who retire later than the base age at which they are eligible for 100 percent of their formula benefits. This is already an inducement to work longer, yet relatively few take advantage of it. Unlike professors and politicians, most Americans prefer to quit their jobs earlier. If the base retirement age were raised, those retiring at the new, higher age would lose their premium, those retiring at the current base age would receive less than 100 percent of the normal benefits, and those retiring at sixty-two would get still less.

A better way to entice workers to delay retirement would be to offer full Social Security benefits to those who continue to work between the ages of sixty-five and sixty-nine; by reducing or eliminating benefits, current law actually discourages older workers from staying on the job. Eliminating the tax on Social Security earnings that kicks in as outside earnings increase would also encourage people to keep working.

Means-testing Social Security benefits, which the budget-balancing Concord Coalition and others strongly advocate, would threaten to undo the system altogether. Benefit formulas are such that people with high incomes during their working years already receive benefits that are proportionately much less than what people with low incomes receive. Further reducing the benefits of the upper middle class and the rich—perhaps eliminating them entirely on the grounds that these folks do not "need" them—would create a widespread perception that Social Security is just another "welfare" program for the poor. That would vastly undermine its current, broad-based support.

In no meaningful sense does Social Security suffer currently from a "deficit." Cutting Social Security benefits now, in any way, in order to balance the federal budget would be particularly reprehensible because, as I have suggested earlier, budget balancing offers no clear benefits. In no case is increasing the burdens on the elderly necessary, justified, or fair.

Most people would like to look forward, as they age, to truly golden years, in which they can live in at least as much, if not greater, ease as in their youth. A rich society like ours can certainly afford to provide such ease.

5

PUTTING ALL THE DEFICITS TOGETHER

Reducing the federal budget deficit—even achieving a "balanced budget"—is hailed in many quarters as a panacea. It would, at least as a matter of accounting (holding other components of the accounts fixed), correspond to an increase in net foreign investment (the net increase of U.S. claims abroad versus foreign claims on this country) and hence to a reduction in our international current account deficit. If, as the budget-balancers argue, it does contribute to economic growth, it will reduce the imagined deficits in Social Security as well. It will accomplish this by generating greater contributions to the trust funds and by increasing the size of the pie upon which future workers and retirees will dine.

Cuts in budget deficits, it is claimed without clear empirical or historical support, would also bring down interest rates. Lower interest rates, if they did materialize, would bring down the exchange rate for the dollar and would, eventually if not immediately, increase exports and discourage imports, shrinking the trade deficit. By stimulating the domestic economy, lower interest rates would further reduce the budget deficit. And a more prosperous economy would also, as indicated, reduce any supposed deficits in Social Security.

But interest rates can be kept down by the Federal Reserve with appropriate monetary policy. Moreover, trimming the relevant cyclically adjusted or structural budget deficits slows the economy by reducing private financial wealth and purchasing power.

Taking direct measures to reduce those perceived Social Security deficits, whether by cutting benefits or increasing taxes, would harm consumer purchasing power. By discouraging purchases of foreign as well as domestic goods and services, such measures would in turn narrow the trade deficit. They would probably also lead to smaller budget deficits, but this effect would be diminished if the reductions in consumer spending slowed the economy.

Reducing or eliminating budget deficits may well trim the trade deficit. But another by-product of such policies, unfortunately, would be weakened economic growth. Since larger inflation- and cyclically adjusted deficits are associated with lower unemployment and faster growth in income and output, slimming these deficits stanches the flow of imports into the United States. If an absolute balance of trade is considered truly paramount, it can always be achieved by creating a recession that cuts sufficiently consumers' ability to spend on anything, including foreign goods.

These issues are all intertwined in the broader questions of intergenerational equity and provision for the future.[1] Budget deficit reduction is presumed by its advocates to raise national saving and thus to increase future consumption opportunities even as it limits consumption today. It thus aids future generations and the current younger generation, which can look forward to a long, prosperous life, at the expense of the older generation substantially with no such prospect.

Reducing deficits in international trade and investment out of concern for the drain on our future resources that servicing U.S. obligations to foreigners represents would diminish the opportunities for current consumption and domestic investment. It, too, benefits the young and future generations at the expense of the old. And reducing the alleged deficits in Social Security, if achieved by cutting benefits, also entails a transfer from older to younger generations.

Rarely considered is the basic issue of whether such intergenerational transfers are justified as a matter of equity, let alone whether they are economically feasible. With regard to the latter, as indicated in the previous section, at any given time everyone alive must be supported by those who are working and producing at that time. The only way to change what is available at any time is to change the quantity (or quality) of productive capital in use at that time. This includes all capital, public and private, human and intangible as well as physical and tangible.

The questions about the practicality of such intergenerational transfers and whether they really push out what economists' jargon calls the "intertemporal production possibility frontier" have not generally been clearly answered. Conservative advocates of a lesser role for government are likely to argue that devoting more resources to public investment will not help; government activities are inherently wasteful and nonproductive. But advocates of free markets may also question whether public policy intended to increase private saving and investment will necessarily raise productivity.

First, measures to increase saving may, if reduced consumption lowers income and output, actually lessen investment and hence saving. The old Keynesian paradox of thrift may, under certain circumstances, be operative. Would the lower interest rates presumably stemming from increased efforts to save offer enough stimulus to investment to counter the depressing effect of lower consumption?

But even if more investment were to be realized, what if business has already carried investment to the point where further capital will add nothing to net product, that is, will add less in terms of productive capacity than its cost?[2] More national saving may then leave us with less consumption now and less consumption in the future as well. It may fail to encourage sufficient future consumption to compensate for the current cost of investing.

A more basic question is whether sacrifice by the current generation in the interest of the future is justified. Is it known that those living in the future will be in greater need than those living now? Is it not likely that, with continued growth in the economy, our children and grandchildren will live much better than we do without any increase in saving? I have noted previously that even a modest 1 percent annual increase in output per worker will raise per capita income by more than a third by the year 2030, and even more as the years go by. Why should people today sacrifice so that those lucky enough to be born later will live still better?

It is extremely difficult to define an "optimal rate of saving," particularly when dealing with saving by one generation or age cohort that is presumed to benefit another. What are the obligations of the old to the young? Have the elderly perhaps helped the young enough by raising them and investing in their education? And if the elderly are to help the young more, is not that better done by raising them better—beginning with prenatal care and going on to improved child care and education at all levels—by better parenting, and by protecting all our children and neighborhoods from poverty, crime, and drugs?

In view of all these considerations, one can hardly argue that budget deficits, particularly as currently measured, should necessarily be reduced, let alone eliminated. Aggressive budget cutting might not be socially desirable even in the uncertain event that it did increase national saving. Similar doubts extend to efforts to slash the trade deficit if these take the form either of slowing the economy or of interfering with free trade at the expense of economic efficiency. And they apply all the more strongly to unfair—indeed unconscionable— efforts to deal with hypothesized Social Security deficits by cutting benefits to the elderly.

There are real deficits in our society. Deficits in the provision of a safe, uplifting environment for all of our citizens. Deficits in education of the young and protection of all from violence. Deficits in preservation and improvement of the country's natural resources of land, water, and air. Our real problems are not the deficits—actual, exaggerated, or alleged—in the federal budget, international trade, and Social Security.

Notes

Chapter 2

1. The hypothesis of "Ricardian equivalence" advanced by Robert Barro suggests that increased wealth in the form of interest-bearing securities will not affect private spending because it will create a public perception of an obligation to service or pay off a debt equal in value to the debt it holds. An extremely voluminous literature has been produced to debate this point, but the weight of the argument and empirical evidence would seem to confirm that this negative counterbalance to the wealth effect of debt held by the public is only partial, if it exists at all.

2. *Budget of the United States Government, Fiscal Year 1998* (Washington, D.C.: U.S. Government Printing Office, 1997), p. 211.

3. *Economic Indicators*, prepared for the Joint Economic Committee of Congress by the Council of Economic Advisers (Washington, D.C.: Government Printing Office, June 1997), p. 33.

4. *Budget of the United States Government, Fiscal Year 1998*, p. 227, Table 12–6.

5. This represents the 73 percent of net interest payments received by Americans, divided by the 1996 population of 265,455,000.

6. Net interest payments as a percentage of GDP are projected to decline from 15.5 percent in 1997 to 13.6 percent in 2002. *Budget of the United States Government, 1998*, p. 217, Table 12.1.

7. The average of the annual rates of growth of nominal GDP from 1993 to 1997 (first quarter to first quarter) was 5.33 percent. From the first quarter of 1996 to the first quarter of 1997 the rate of growth was 6.24 percent.

8. Maintenance of the 0.43 percent deficit/GDP ratio would reduce the debt/GDP ratio to 8.6 percent. All this can be confirmed with a pocket calculator or, for those so inclined, by exploring the following bit of algebra, largely reproduced from Robert Eisner, *The Misunderstood Economy: What Counts and How to Count It* (Boston: Harvard Business School Press, 1994).

The differential for the change in the debt/GDP ratio, symbolized as B/Y, is

$$\Delta(B/Y) = (Y\Delta B - B\Delta Y)/Y^2 = \Delta B/Y - (B/Y)(\Delta Y/Y).$$

For the debt/GDP ratio to stay the same, the debt must grow at the same rate as GDP, or $\Delta B/B = \Delta Y/Y$; substituting $\Delta B/B$ for $\Delta Y/Y$ sets the equation above to zero. But the deficit (D) equals the change in the debt ($D = \Delta B$). More generally, then,

$$\Delta(B/Y) \gtreqless 0 \text{ as } D/Y \gtreqless (B/Y)(\Delta Y/Y);$$

in words, the debt/GDP ratio increases, decreases, or stays the same as the deficit ratio is greater than, less than, or equal to the product of the debt ratio and the rate of growth of GDP.

For a constant debt-GDP ratio the equation is

$$\Delta(B/Y) = D/Y - (B/Y)(\Delta Y/Y) = 0, \text{ whence}$$
$$B/Y = D/Y \div \Delta Y/Y;$$

that is, the equilibrium or "balanced" debt/GDP ratio equals the deficit/GDP ratio divided by the rate of growth of GDP. A lower deficit/GDP ratio will lower the debt/GDP ratio. A permanently higher deficit ratio will not raise the debt/GDP ratio indefinitely; it will only raise it to a new, higher equilibrium. And a higher rate of growth of GDP will lower the equilibrium debt/GDP ratio.

9. It is clear that the Fed can affect short-term rates, which are relevant to much of the Treasury debt. Long-term rates are as a first approximation the average of expected future short-term rates. They will hence move in the same direction as short-term rates if investors are convinced that the Fed will persist in a low-rate policy. Some argue, with little supporting evidence, that the lower short-term rates will spark fears of an "overheated" economy that will increase inflation. The expectation of more inflation would then raise long-term

interest rates. But even this would leave real rates; that is, nominal rates minus expected inflation, no higher and probably lower since the evidence here is that nominal interest rates do not in fact rise as much as inflation. Thus, with higher nominal long-term rates due to greater inflation there would still tend to be more investment.

10. This follows from modern theories of the consumption function stemming from independent work by Nobel laureates Franco Modigliani and Milton Friedman, supported by a wealth of empirical studies. Principles of portfolio choice and asset balance indicate that business and other nonfederal investment will also be promoted by increases in the proportions of financial wealth.

11. See Robert Eisner, *How Real Is the Federal Deficit?* (New York: Free Press, 1986), as well as a number of subsequent works, for a full discussion of this issue.

12. Robert Eisner and Sang-In Hwang, "Self-Correcting Real Deficits: A New Lesson in Functional Finance," in *The Political Economy of Government Debt*, ed. Harrie A. A. Verban and Frans A. A. M. Van Winden (Amsterdam: North Holland, 1993), pp. 255–94.

13. Named after James Tobin of Yale University and Robert Mundell of Columbia University, who first pointed it out.

14. See Robert Eisner, "Our NAIRU Limit: The Governing Myth of Economic Policy," *American Prospect*, Spring 1995, pp. 58–63; Robert Eisner, "The Retreat from Full Employment," in *Employment, Economic Growth and the Tyranny of the Market: Essays in Honour of Paul Davidson*, vol. 2, ed. Philip Arestis (Brookfield, Vt.: Edward Elgar Publishing Co., 1996), pp. 106–30; Robert Eisner, "Deficits and Unemployment," in *Reclaiming Prosperity: A Blueprint for Progressive Economic Reform* (Washington, D.C.: Economic Policy Institute, 1996), pp. 27–38; Robert Eisner, "A New View of the NAIRU," in *Improving the Global Economy: Keynesianism and the Growth in Output and Employment*, ed. P. Davidson and J. Kregel (Brookfield, Vt.: Edward Elgar Publishing Co., October 1997); and Robert Eisner, "The Decline and Fall of the NAIRU," presented to the American Economic Association annual meeting, New Orleans, January 1997.

15. See, for example, Olivier Blanchard, "Unemployment: Getting the Questions Right and Some of the Answers," in *Europe's Unemployment Problem*, ed. J. H. Drèze and C. R. Bean (Cambridge, Mass.: MIT Press, 1990); James Tobin, "The Natural Rate as New Classical Economics," in *The Natural Rate of Unemployment:*

Reflections on 25 Years of the Hypothesis, ed. Rod Cross (New York: Cambridge University Press, 1995); Frank Hahn, "Theoretical Reflections on the 'Natural Rate of Unemployment'," in Cross, *Natural Rate of Unemployment*; Rod Cross, "Is the Natural Rate Hypothesis Consistent with Hysteresis?" in Cross, *Natural Rate of Unemployment*; Ray C. Fair, "Testing the Standard View of the Long-Run Unemployment-Inflation Relationship," Cowles Foundation, Yale University, March 1996; Ray C. Fair, "Testing the NAIRU Model for 27 Countries" and "Testing the NAIRU Model for the United States," Cowles Foundation, Yale University, March 1997; Douglas Staiger, James H. Stock, and Mark W. Watson, "The NAIRU, Unemployment and Monetary Policy," *Journal of Economic Perspectives* 11, no. 1 (Winter 1997): 33–49; Olivier Blanchard and Lawrence F. Katz, "What We Know and Do Not Know about the Natural Rate of Unemployment," *Journal of Economic Perspectives* 11, no. 1 (Winter 1997): 51–72; Richard Rogerson, "Theory Ahead of Language in the Economics of Unemployment," *Journal of Economic Perspectives* 11, no. 1 (Winter 1997): 73–92; and James K. Galbraith, "Time to Ditch the NAIRU," *Journal of Economic Perspectives* 11, no. 1 (Winter 1997): 93–108. See also James K. Galbraith's forthcoming Twentieth Century Fund book on inequality, to be published by the Free Press.

16. Robert J. Gordon, "The Time-Varying NAIRU and Its Implications for Economic Policy," *Journal of Economic Perspectives* 11, no. 1 (Winter 1997): 11–32.

17. Gordon bases his calculations of inflation on the CPI (consumer price index).

18. Eisner, *How Real Is the Federal Deficit?*; Robert Eisner and Paul J. Pieper, "Deficits, Monetary Policy and Real Economic Activity" in *The Economics of Public Debt*, ed. Kenneth J. Arrow and Michael J. Boskin (London: Macmillan, 1988), pp. 3–40; Robert Eisner, "Sense and Nonsense about Budget Deficits," *Harvard Business Review*, May/June 1993, pp. 99–111; Eisner, *Misunderstood Economy*; Robert Eisner, "U.S. National Saving and Budget Deficits," in *Macroeconomic Policy after the Conservative Era*, ed. Gerald A. Epstein and Herbert Gintis (New York: Cambridge University Press, 1995), pp. 109–42; and Robert Eisner, "National Saving and Budget Deficits," *Review of Economics and Statistics* 76, no. 1 (February 1994): 181–86.

19. The relationship is confirmed in an ordinary least squares regression, over the years 1967 to 1996, of changes in unemployment on the

previous 4-percent-unemployment, inflation-adjusted surplus. The regression coefficient was a highly significant 0.49, with a standard error of 0.12. This indicates that on the average each percentage point more of deficit was associated with about half of one percent reduction of unemployment

The value of R-Square was 0.39, indicating that a substantial portion of the variance of changes in unemployment was explained by the previous cyclically and inflation-adjusted deficit but, of course, a substantial amount was not. My previous work has indicated that variables reflecting monetary policy and exchange rates added to the explanation. For those wondering how the deficit-unemployment relation I report is consistent with recent declining unemployment in the face of reductions in deficits, the explanation is not hard to find. There is the impact of these other variables and the momentum of major forces such as the high-tech information boom of the last several years. But further, the actual deficit has virtually disappeared in large part because of relatively high employment and more rapid growth. The *cyclically and inflation-adjusted* deficit has come down very little. This deficit has its impact with a lag of at least a year and for 1996 its previous value, measured at 4 percent unemployment, was 0.60 percent of GDP, actually higher than the value of 0.22 percent for 1989.

20. Eisner, "U.S. National Saving and Budget Deficits," p. 131, Table 4.7.

21. See ibid., pp. 126–27, Table 4.6; Eisner, "National Saving and Budget Deficits," p. 183, Table 1.

22. The 27 percent of interest payments made by the Treasury to foreign holders of the U.S. debt are also generally put back into circulation by these foreign holders, who make new investments in dollar assets or purchase American goods.

23. Depreciation charges are an average of past capital outlays. In a growing economy, and with growing firms, current outlays are almost always larger than this average of past outlays. This disparity is magnified considerably by inflation. As a consequence of these factors, depreciation or capital consumption allowances in the private economy are only about two-thirds of current capital expenditures.

24. Perhaps because it is better in tax management terms to charge expenses as they are incurred rather than to amortize them over time, businesses also, unfortunately, follow the accounting convention of not capitalizing research and development expenditures that are excluded from investment in fixed capital.

25. Of course, capital investment, private as well as public, can be excessive. Tax incentives and subsidies that induce business to invest unwisely or more than would be profitable under conditions of full employment are best avoided. Resources may well have been wasted on half-empty shopping centers and office buildings, on misguided investment in steel capacity, and on nuclear power plants that proved uneconomical. Public investment can also be misguided, although there is increasing evidence that, in general, the largely public investment in infrastructure and particularly in human capital has had a high payoff.

26. By Charles Schultze of the Brookings Institution, former head of the Budget Bureau under President Johnson and chairman of President Carter's Council of Economic Advisers.

Chapter 3

1. In fact, trade deficits fluctuate; the latest figures available showed a decline.

2. The problems of measurement are such that when one adds up all reported exports of all nations and then adds up the reported imports, the totals are not equal. World imports appear to exceed world exports. This means that nations on the whole tend to find themselves in what seems to be deficit, making efforts to achieve balance or export surpluses all the more frustrating. The reasons for the discrepancies have to do with the fact that many countries with tariffs, import controls, or other regulations on goods coming in tend to keep a fuller count of their imports, while less attention is paid to exports.

3. The famed, or infamous, Smoot-Hawley tariff in the United States, passed despite its widespread condemnation by economists, was perhaps the worst of these.

4. Or to some extent foreigners may reacquire their own currencies, if Americans deplete what balances they have in them, thus reducing U.S. gross and net claims on the rest of the world.

5. See Robert Eisner and Paul J. Pieper, "The World's Greatest Debtor Nation?" *North American Review of Economics and Finance* 1, no. 1 (1990): 9–32. The Bureau of Economic Analysis subsequently incorporated similar estimates of changes in values of claims in their analyses of the international investment position.

6. *Federal Reserve Bulletin*, June 1997, p. A27, Table 1.41.

7. Bureau of Economic Analysis, U.S. Department of Commerce, *Survey of Current Business*, July 1997, p. 31.

8. Further, past declines in the dollar have to a considerable extent been absorbed by foreign sellers who, anxious not to lose their American markets, refrained from raising prices to match their losses on the dollar.

9. China Ministry of Foreign Trade and Economic Cooperation, as cited in *Chicago Tribune*, September 15, 1977. The Chinese have been using much of their surplus to accumulate claims on foreign currencies, giving them the largest such reserves in the world. I view this as a dubious prudence, a curious throwback to the mercantilist doctrine mentioned earlier. China might be wiser to reduce its surplus and run down these reserves as it opens its markets to more imports, particularly imports of the capital goods that would help it maintain its phenomenal growth of recent years.

Chapter 4

1. Substantial parts of this section were presented in a lecture, "Don't Sock the Elderly, Help Them; Old Age Is Hard Enough," presented at the University of Illinois Law School, February 11, 1997, to be published in *Elder Law Journal* 5, no. 2. Parts were originally prepared for the author's editorial page article, "What Social Security Crisis?" *Wall Street Journal*, August 30, 1996, or for a letter to the *Wall Street Journal* printed on March 28, 1997.

2. See *1997 Annual Report of the Board of Trustees of the Federal Old-Age and Survivors Insurance and Disability Insurance Trust Funds* (hereafter referred to as *OASDI 1997 Annual Report*), p. 5.

3. Ibid., p. 6.

4. *1997 Annual Report of the Board of Trustees of the Federal Supplementary Medical Insurance Trust Fund*, p. 5.

5. *OASDI 1997 Annual Report*, pp. 13–15, 26, 54–65.

6. Ibid., p. 148, Table II.H1.

7. Calculated as $100 \times (1 - 1/1.0498) = 4.74$ percent.

8. The monthly benefit database maintained by the Office of the Chief Actuary of the Social Security Administration put the average monthly figure for 1996 at $792.66.

9. Fact Sheet no. 52, Public Policy Institute, Washington, D.C., September 1996, Table 3.

10. Daniel B. Radner, "Family Unit Incomes of the Elderly and Children, 1994," ORES Working Paper no. 70, Office of Research, Evaluation and Statistics, Social Security Administration, November 1996.

11. *Social Security Reform: The Basics* (New York: Twentieth Century Fund Press, 1996).

Chapter 5

1. There has been considerable attention in recent years to "generational accounting," largely the work of Laurence Kotlikoff of Boston University and Alan Auerbach, now at the University of California, Berkeley. They have portrayed a fiscal system that is offering benefits to "current generations" at prospectively great expense to "future generations," who would face huge tax rates to meet the obligations now being imposed on them.

I have a number of objections to the conclusions of the Kotlikoff-Auerbach analysis, based on its special, specific assumptions. For one thing, the interest payments on the debt to be made in the future are judged a burden but not, for the 70 percent or more of these payments that will be received in the United States, a benefit. Second, the analysis does not take into account the fact that current public investment offers future benefits. Third, in arriving at the astronomical amount of tax increases on those future generations, their studies assume that none of the increases will be shared by those currently alive. "Future generations" are taken literally to include only those not yet born. Thus, if in twenty years it were found necessary to increase taxes, the increases would fall only on those born in 2017 and later. Would an implicit "grandfather clause" protect everybody else from the greater tax burden? Finally, and most fundamentally, the Kotlikoff-Auerbach analysis restricts itself to public fiscal accounting rather than the ultimately relevant measure of how well-off in all respects each generation is likely to be.

Comprehensive generational accounting can well be useful. But it should go far beyond the narrow examination of taxes and transfers under restrictive assumptions. Rather, it should cover the intergenerational or broadly intertemporal distribution of all capital and income—public and private, intangible and tangible, market and non-market—discussed in part in the text above.

2. The correct, strict test should be to determine whether that net product is greater than its cost after taking into account that a dollar of future product is worth less presently valued than a dollar of current investment cost.

INDEX

Smoot-Hawley tariff, 66 *n*3
Social Security benefits, 1–2,
    31–32, 50–51, 54–55
Social Security deficits, 44; finan-
    cing, 44–46; myths, 43–44, 45,
    54; reducing, 57, 58
Spending. *See* Consumption;
    Government spending
Standard of living, 44, 51
State constitutions, 4
Stein, Herbert, 18
Supply and demand, 36, 39. *See
    also* Demand (for goods and
    services)

Tariffs, 31
Taxes, 7, 8, 15, 18, 20, 26. *See
    also* Income taxes; Payroll
    taxes
Terms of trade, 38, 39
Trade, 31, 36, 38–39, 57
Trade deficits, 22, 29, 39, 41;
    impact on, 1, 58; measuring,

33, 66 *n*2; portrayal of,
    30–31; reducing, 36, 40, 57.
    See also Current account
    deficit
Trade policies, 29–30, 39
Trade surplus, 29, 30
Trust funds, 1, 4, 43, 44, 45–46

Unemployment, 1, 18, 20–21,
    46, 48; impact of trade on,
    29–30, 38–39; reducing, 22,
    25, 34, 58
Unilateral transfers, 22, 31–32

Value of assets, 32–33, 34

Wealth, 61 *n*1
Wealth-to-income ratio, 15
World trade, 30, 31

Zero-sum game, 30

ABOUT THE AUTHOR

Robert Eisner, professor emeritus of economics at Northwestern University, is a past president of the American Economic Association. He is a fellow of the American Academy of Arts and Sciences and the Econometric Society. He has published extensively in professional and academic journals and writes frequent columns on economic affairs for the *Wall Street Journal*, *Los Angeles Times*, and other general media. His previous books include *The Misunderstood Economy: What Counts and How to Count It*, *How Real Is the Federal Deficit?* and *The Total Incomes System of Accounts*.